ROUTLEDGE LIBRARY EDITIONS: ACCOUNTING HISTORY

Volume 2

THE ACCOUNTANT'S MAGAZINE

THE ACCOUNTANT'S MAGAZINE
An Anthology

Edited by
COLIN STORRAR

Routledge
Taylor & Francis Group
LONDON AND NEW YORK

First published in 1986 by Garland Publishing, Inc.

This edition first published in 2021
by Routledge
2 Park Square, Milton Park, Abingdon, Oxon OX14 4RN

and by Routledge
52 Vanderbilt Avenue, New York, NY 10017

Routledge is an imprint of the Taylor & Francis Group, an informa business

© 1986 Colin Storrar

All rights reserved. No part of this book may be reprinted or reproduced or utilised in any form or by any electronic, mechanical, or other means, now known or hereafter invented, including photocopying and recording, or in any information storage or retrieval system, without permission in writing from the publishers.

Trademark notice: Product or corporate names may be trademarks or registered trademarks, and are used only for identification and explanation without intent to infringe.

British Library Cataloguing in Publication Data
A catalogue record for this book is available from the British Library

ISBN: 978-0-367-33564-9 (Set)
ISBN: 978-1-00-304636-3 (Set) (ebk)
ISBN: 978-0-367-53339-7 (Volume 2) (hbk)
ISBN: 978-0-367-53347-2 (Volume 2) (pbk)
ISBN: 978-1-00-308147-0 (Volume 2) (ebk)

Publisher's Note
The publisher has gone to great lengths to ensure the quality of this reprint but points out that some imperfections in the original copies may be apparent.

Disclaimer
The publisher has made every effort to trace copyright holders and would welcome correspondence from those they have been unable to trace.

THE ACCOUNTANT'S MAGAZINE
An Anthology

Colin Storrar, editor

Garland Publishing, Inc.
New York and London
1986

For a complete list of Garland's publications in accounting, please see the final pages of this volume.

Copyright © 1986 by Colin Storrar

Library of Congress Cataloging-in-Publication Data

The Accountant's magazine.

(Accounting thought and practice through the years)
A selection of articles from the Accountant's magazine for the years between 1897 and 1954.
"Published on behalf of the Scottish Committee on Accounting History of the Institute of Chartered Accountants of Scotland"—P.
Includes index.
1. Accounting. 2. Accounting—Scotland. I. Storrar, Colin. II. Scottish Committee on Accounting History. III. Accountant's magazine. IV. Series.
HF5629.A252 1986   657   86-9953
ISBN 0-8240-7872-1

Design by Bonnie Goldsmith

The volumes in this series are printed on acid-free, 250-year-life paper.

*This book has been published on behalf of
the Scottish Committee on Accounting History
of the Institute of Chartered Accountants of Scotland.*

ACKNOWLEDGMENT AND COMMENT

Grateful thanks are extended to the editor of *The Accountant's Magazine* for permission to reproduce the items in this anthology. The original idea for an anthology came from Tom Robertson, a founding member of the Scottish Accounting History Committee who was unable to complete the project due to his death in 1981.

Contents

Introduction

J. Haldane, "Eminent Accountants of the Past, III: Donald Lindsay," August 1897, pp. 495–99.	3
Unsigned, "The Treatment of Bad and Doubtful Debts," May 1898, pp. 272–76.	8
Editorial, "Income Tax," July 1903, pp. 365–68.	13
N.J.D. Kennedy, "The Relation of Auditors to Public Companies," December 1904, pp. 534–51.	18
F. Tod, "Cost Accounts," August 1905, pp. 439–46.	37
Editorial, "Edinburgh University and Accountant Students," June 1906, pp. 287–90.	45
J. B. Macdonald, "Capital and Revenue Accounts: Their Origin and Nature: The Genesis of the Double-Account System," February 1907, pp. 116–21.	50
Unsigned, "The Twenty-First Annual Meeting of the American Association of Public Accountants: Impressions of a Visitor," December 1908, pp. 552–59.	56
Unsigned, "Counting by Electricity," April 1913, pp. 196–99.	64
Editor, "Intimations and Reports: Society of Accountants in Edinburgh," March 1917, pp. 144–49.	68
H. R., "The Apprentice in the Army," December 1918, pp. 464–65.	74
H. R., "The Apprentice Returned," August 1919, pp. 412–13.	76

C. H. Temple, "The Accountants Relationship with the Inland Revenue," March 1924, pp. 192–96.   78

Editorial, "Verification of Assets," November 1924, pp. 591–93.   83

W. T. Baxter, extract dealing with the Harvard Business School, from "American Universities and the Teaching of Commerce," November 1933, pp. 608–09 and pp. 615–19.   86

W. F. Eva, "The Dunlop Rubber Company Accounts," June 1934, pp. 353–58.   95

C. R. Curtis, "The Accountant and the Machine," November 1936, pp. 565–70.   101

I. W. Macdonald, "Principles Underlying Profit Statements and Balance-Sheets," November 1938, pp. 539–50.   107

H.C.F. Holgate, "Accountancy Must Look Forward," May 1942, pp. 210–11.   120

T. Robinson, "Tax Avoidance," February 1944, pp. 82–85.   122

Editorial, "Public Ownership for the Steel Industry," June 1946, pp. 217–18.   126

R. Taylor, "Budgetary Control and Standard Costs," December 1946, pp. 417–25.   129

F.R.M. de Paula, "The Effects of the Price Level on Accounting," November 1952, pp. 357–64.   139

A Member, "Summer School Impressions," August 1953, pp. 414–19.   148

H. E. Wincott, "Interpretation of Company Accounts," April 1954, pp. 205–13.   155

INTRODUCTION

The Scottish Societies of Chartered Accountants

The Accountants' Magazine (*TAM*) was first published in January 1897. At that date the Scottish professional men known as chartered accountants comprised members of three separate bodies, incorporated by royal charter: the Society of Accountants in Edinburgh (founded 1854), the Institute of Accountants and Actuaries in Glasgow (founded 1855), and the Society of Accountants in Aberdeen (founded 1867).

These bodies were similar in organization. Each admitted only male candidates who had attained an accepted standard of secondary education and had then been apprenticed for several years to members in public practice. One of the few differences related to the apprenticeship premium paid to the practitioner by his apprentices at the commencement of their service, a practice that endured in Edinburgh after it had ceased in Glasgow.

University graduate entrants to the Scottish profession were few. But all other apprentices were obliged to attend specified university classes, at first only in law but subsequently also in economics and accountancy when these subjects were offered by the universities in the three cities concerned.

Until 1951 *TAM* was published on behalf of the three Scottish accounting bodies. However, with their amalgamation in 1951 to form the present Institute of Chartered Accountants of Scotland, it became the official journal of the institute. It is now issued to all members and students and used as the vehicle for council statements.

The first editor of *TAM* was Richard Brown, a practitioner, secretary of the Edinburgh Society, and author of *A History of Accounting and Accountants*, published in 1905 to mark the golden jubilee of the society. The longest-serving was Adam G. Murray, editor from 1922 until 1952, a practitioner and professor (part-time) at the University of Edinburgh.

During the period 1897 to 1951 *TAM* was one of the two main links binding the three bodies, the other being the General Examining Board. Although *TAM* reported the meetings and pronouncements of the separate bodies, editorial policy emphasized the common features of the Scottish profession and encouraged the use of the term "Scottish chartered accountant." Few differences of opinion among the bodies were reported in *TAM* in the course of almost sixty years. One such difference was the presumed greater enthusiasm in Glasgow for the admission of women members in the years following the First World War.

TAM editorials had long urged the establishment of commercial studies at Scottish universities (see Item 6), and in 1911 one such editorial advocated as "the ideal system" one "where the professional man should receive the whole of the necessary instruction in theory and principles at a university." *TAM* duly applauded the decision to institute a commerce degree at Edinburgh (1917) and published the inaugural lecture by Professor Laird—a member of the Edinburgh Society. However, university education was not to be a substitute for practical work but a complement to it. That this opinion was applied to other than accountancy students is illustrated by a 1930 editorial that urged universities to "develop their commercial education on more practical lines than at present" and not to award degrees to students "without practical experience." Against this background of support for university accounting education, albeit of a highly vocational nature, the future professor Baxter's account of the teaching of commerce at American universities, and his description of the case-study system already well established at the Harvard Business School, is particularly interesting (Item 15).

When *TAM* was first issued, the Edinburgh and Glasgow bodies had been in existence for over forty years, and the Aberdeen Society for almost thirty. It was the journal not of a new profession but of one in the process of consolidating its position. That profession had existed since long before the issue of the first charter in 1854, and amongst the early contents of *TAM* are to be found biographical sketches of prominent accountants of the past (for example, Item 1). These are not obituaries, but historical sketches; thus Donald Lindsay, the subject of the note reproduced in the anthology, had died over twenty years previously.

As we have seen, the Scottish Institute was created in 1951 by the amalgamation of the three previous accounting bodies. In order to preserve continuity with the past, the merger arrangements provided for the members of the Glasgow and Aberdeen bodies to be admitted to the Edinburgh Society, which then changed its name to The Institute of Chartered Accountants of Scotland. An early fruit of these amalgamations was the introduction in 1953 of the present series of summer schools held at the University of St. Andrews. The blend of theory, practice, and golf then established is captured in the description of that first occasion by an anonymous member (Item 24).

From its earliest issues *TAM* was in favor of the federation, although not amalgamation, of the professional societies of accountants within the UK and to some extent elsewhere in the British Empire and even the US. In practice, however, the Scottish bodies strove to defend their position both against the pretensions of The Institute of Chartered Accountants in England and Wales—then, as more recently, perceived as inclined to forget that it had no mandate to speak for the UK accountancy profession—and other bodies thought to be attempting to obtain part of the birthright of chartered accountants by the use of names or initials too close to the designated membership label "C. A." of the three Scottish chartered bodies. This combination of views led to an editorial scepticism regarding the virtues of state registration of the profession, an objective advanced from time to time by advocates outside Scotland. The usual editorial opinion appeared to be that the immediate dilution of the status of chartered accountants might not be offset by the future benefits accruing to a united profession of public accountants. One plea for a unified and democratically controlled profession (Item 19) was made at the height of the Second World War by H.C.F. Holgate, a frequent contributor to *TAM*.

Background Events

Our period coincides with that often regarded as encompassing the decline of the UK from a position at the center of a world empire to one of uneasy dependence on the US whilst hovering on the fringe of a Europe recovering from the devastation of the Second World War. With one major exception there is little direct reflection of these great events in the first nineteen volumes of *TAM*, which imply a world normally at peace, where stable prices were taken for granted, the level of international trade steadily expanded, and former colonies became self-governing without breaking their commercial and cultural ties with the UK. There are many editorial references to the formation and progress of societies of accountants overseas, particularly in the self-governing dominions and the US. Meetings of the new societies in Australia, for example, are reported similarly to those in England and Ireland, while the visit of the editor to the twenty-first annual meeting of the American Association of Public Accountants in 1908 is reported at length (Item 8).

The collapse of this stable and optimistic world occurred during the First World War. At first, the reporting of the effects of war was limited to the publication of lists of members, apprentices, and staff entering the armed forces and technical articles on such topics as war taxation and the legal position of enemy aliens. Gradually, however, war casualties and the absence of recruits to the public accountancy profession brought about a change. The list of casualties published in November 1916, for example, contains the names of fifteen dead, fourteen wounded, and four missing. A postwar editorial gives some idea of the extent of involvement in the war effort—of a total membership of 564, 172 members of the Edinburgh Society served in the armed forces, of whom 28 were killed; in addition, 225 apprentices served, of whom 48 were killed. The atmosphere of the time is illustrated by the report of the 1917 annual meeting of the Edinburgh Society (Item 10), when, for the first time, the total membership had actually decreased.

Towards the end of the war much editorial attention was given to the problem of re-integrating returned servicemen into the profession and to the future position of women who had largely replaced male assistants during the war years. It was believed that the charters of the three Scottish bodies denied membership to women, and there was thought to be continuing opposition to their entry. Moves toward amending the charters were soon rendered irrelevant, however, by the Sex Disqualification Bill, and during the 1920s the three bodies began to admit and, indeed, welcome women members. In a lighter vein, the changes brought about during the war years are discussed in two very brief articles: "The Apprentice in the Army" and "The Apprentice Returned" (Items 11 and 12), published soon after cessation of the war.

In the years between the two World Wars *TAM* articles ranged over a variety of subjects of interest to accountants and businessmen—for example, it was proposed that accountants could act as potential arbiters between capital and labor. Other articles dealt with such contemporary economic problems as war debts and the need to return to "sound money." In addition, several articles on the life of Scottish chartered accountants overseas were published at this time. In contrast to such prewar pieces as "The Anglo-Indian Accountant—His Social Life," which were essentially travel writing, those of the 1920s set out to inform young men about the career prospects, salaries, and working conditions to be expected in the accountancy professions of various countries.

The years of and following the Second World War evidenced a marked change of editorial attitude toward the world outside. This is perhaps surprising since the editor (A. G. Murray) had held his position since the 1920s. During the war, editorials were published with such titles as "The US and World Civilisation" and "When the Red Army Reaches Berlin." This dramatic expansion of editorial horizons to embrace grand strategy could be explained by the overwhelming importance to the UK and its citizens of a successful outcome to the war. When the triumph of the Allied cause was assured, however, editorial attention did not return to matters of narrowly professional interest. Instead, editorials displayed a novel degree of political partisanship in their criticism of the policies of the 1945–51 Labour government. Thus, the 1946 editorial "Public Ownership for the Steel Industry" (Item 21) accuses the then government of treating Parliament with contempt. The piece is written in a manner more typical of a political weekly than of a formerly sober professional journal. However, in the final volumes of our period the editorials revert to more traditional material.

Technical Topics

In the first issue of *TAM* the editor expressed the intention "to provide a practical business journal for practical business men." The principal place was to be occupied by "the science of clearly keeping, stating and accurately verifying Accounts," but other subjects were to be considered "in their relation to practical affairs." *TAM* intended to follow "all good Accountants" in showing "familiarity with practical law without being lawyers; intimate knowledge of the practices of commerce though not merchants; skill in computation while not professional actuaries; and intelligent interest in monetary and economic questions without claiming to be financiers or political economists."

On the whole, successive editors held to this policy. Throughout the period covered, the majority of the contents of *TAM* comprised material considered relevant to the profession of accountancy, whether for the general information of members, guidance of practitioners, or education of apprentices. These contributions may be classified into the following broad categories: mercantile law, economics, financial accounting and reporting, auditing, cost accounting, personal and company taxation, trust law and accounting, accounting theory, accounting machines and equipment, interpretation of accounts and investment policy, investigations, reconstructions, and amalgamations; and miscellaneous (including examination papers and suggested solutions).

Over the years the relative space devoted to these subjects changed, reflecting, after an interval, their importance to accountants (particularly public accountants). By the date of the first issue the Scottish practicing profession no longer looked to trust and insolvency work as its main occupation. Although not yet compulsory, the professional audit of both public companies and local authorities had become common. It is from this period that the long article on the audit of public companies is taken (Item 4). It has frequently been said of early UK books on auditing that they are dominated by the legal decisions affecting auditors' methods and responsibilities, and this article (a published lecture to a students' society by the professor of law at Aberdeen) is in that tradition. A second item on auditing, dated some twenty years later (Item 14), again emphasizes the importance of judicial decisions in determining the scope of auditors' duties, but goes on to discuss the perennial dilemma of the auditor of a company whose management is dominated by an autocratic director, but who fears to disclose his criticisms to the shareholders.

The sole example of the relatively few articles on bookkeeping (Item 2), which appeared in 1898, advocates the (to us) traditional practice of creating a provision for doubtful debts.

The earliest mention of income tax as a subject of professional concern to public accountants is in a 1903 editorial (Item 3), but the relative paucity of references to taxation before 1914 confirms that taxation as a major preoccupation of public accountants dates from the First World War, when greatly increased rates of personal income tax were imposed. Certainly by the early 1920s taxation was a frequent topic in *TAM*, appearing as reported legal decisions, answers to readers' queries, and articles dealing with the accountant's duties as tax agent (Item 13). The final taxation example appeared during the Second World War at a time when tax avoidance was regarded as much as a sin as a crime (Item 20).

Cost accounting made a first appearance in the Edwardian volumes of *TAM* (Item 5), although it was viewed primarily from the viewpoint of the public accountant seeking to advise manufacturing clients. The other such article, "Budgetary Control and Standard Costs" (Item 22), appeared over forty years later and is representative of the very different world following the Second World War, in which to be American is equated with being modern and efficient.

Another topic for which two contrasting articles have been selected is commentary on published financial statements. The earlier dates from a time when "investment notes" appeared regularly in *TAM* and takes the form of a favorable critique of the 1933 consolidated financial statements of Dunlop Rubber Company Ltd. (Item 16). These statements were issued at a time when consolidated accounts were rarely seen in the UK, and the commentator presents them as an example to others. The second piece is a published lecture (Item 25) given to the Edinburgh students' society in 1954 by H. E. Wincott, a well-known financial journalist of that time. He gives an interesting account of the approach of contemporary analysts, which is notable for the author's anticipation of the conclusions of later research into the efficiency of capital markets.

Accounting principles, broadly defined, form the subject matter of three articles. The first (Item 7) is itself in part a commentary on another article and deals with the distinction between capital and revenue. The second comprises the inaugural public lecture (Item 18) given by Professor Macdonald of the University of Glasgow and probably represents the first occasion on which "accounting principles" (in the modern sense of the term) were discussed in *TAM*. The final example in this section is a 1952 paper (Item 23) on the inflation problem—that is at a time at which the postwar debate on inflation accounting was most active. The paper anticipates many of the points raised again in our own time.

Items under the final heading, dealing with accounting machines and other equipment, appeared at intervals in *TAM*, the earliest being the 1913 article on punched-card equipment (Item 9), which was then in use for the processing of census returns and was "being adopted by railway companies and industrial firms for the preparation of commercial statistics." The 1936 article (Item 17) deals with the effect on audit testing of machine accounting systems and anticipates certain points that were to arise again with the introduction of the office computer by a later generation.

Summary

The twenty-five pieces selected occupy approximately 150 pages, well under one percent of the total contents of the fifty-eight volumes published during the years 1897 to 1954. They do not, of course, form a representative sample of the contents, but rather represent those items that hindsight has shown to possess some enduring significance, either as illustrating the circumstances of a past age or, more commonly, as the vanguard of a coming one. Another important consideration has been brevity. Many of the early technical articles were published lectures given to students' societies and were extremely long by modern standards. Thus, for example, an article published in 1902 under the perennially interesting title "What is Money?" by J. S. Nicholson (a professor of political economy) occupied sixty pages and appeared in four monthly installments.

As suggested above, the early volumes of *TAM* should be of interest to modern accountants, both because nineteenth-century Scotland was the birthplace of organized public accounting and since *TAM*, as the joint production of a fragmented profession, played a unique part in welding together that profession. At the end of the first year of publication the editor of *TAM* reiterated his objective, which was not "to provide amusement for a vacant hour" but "to furnish matter . . . of permanent value [on] everything having relation to business affairs." The readers of the 1980s should decide how far he and his successors attained this aim.

THE ACCOUNTANT'S MAGAZINE
An Anthology

EMINENT ACCOUNTANTS OF THE PAST.

III. DONALD LINDSAY.

DONALD LINDSAY was born in the year 1796; he was a younger son of James Lindsay, who, on his succession to the estate of Boysack in the county of Forfar, assumed the surname of Lindsay-Carnegie.

Mr Lindsay came from his home in Forfarshire to push his fortune in Edinburgh, along with his elder brother, John Mackenzie Lindsay. Both brothers learned business in the office of Mr Alexander Pearson, Writer to the Signet, of the firm of Pearson & Robertson; and John having elected to be a Writer to the Signet, it was probably thought a good variety for Donald to become an accountant. It was at this time that Mr Donald Lindsay formed a close, and what turned out to be a lifelong, friendship with Mr Frederick Fotheringham, who afterwards, with Mr John Lindsay, formed the partnership of Fotheringham & Lindsay, Writers to the Signet, now represented by the firm of Lindsay, Howe, & Co. Mr Fotheringham and Mr Donald Lindsay were typical but not identical examples of a class of Scottish gentlemen more common in former days than in the present generation. The younger sons of good families, they sought and found their fortunes in the professional life of Edinburgh, helped a little by their connection, but more by their own character and talents. The county of Angus, from which they both came in the days before railways, had retained more than might have been expected, from its actual distance from Edinburgh, of the old Scottish character, and manners and customs; many of its natives never left the county, and some of the best of Dean Ramsay's stories are taken from their sayings and doings. But it was a good old Scottish custom for younger sons of the lairds to go early into commerce, trade, and the various professions—the bar being generally reserved for the eldest son. Mr Fotheringham and the Lindsays chummed together as young men, and after Mr John Lindsay's marriage Mr Donald Lindsay and Mr Fotheringham, neither of whom married, continued to live together till nearly the close of their joint lives—a rare instance of close friendship. As illustrative of the old Scottish character, an incident which occurred later in Mr Lindsay's life may be mentioned. Mr Lindsay paid a visit to Rome and brought back with him a collection of copies of the old masters, which were viewed with much concern by a servant, Mary Urquhart, who accompanied Mr Lindsay from Forfarshire to Edinburgh, and who remained an attached inmate of his house till the day of his death. On his return from Rome, Mary called on an old lady, a friend of the family, and told her that it was just terrible that Mr Donald, at his time of life too, had brought home pictures in which the women represented were, she intended to imply, not clothed in that warm and comfortable manner which Scottish climate required, and which Mary's primness deemed requisite and proper.

Mr Lindsay's name appears for the first time among "Accountants in Edinburgh" in Oliver & Boyd's Almanac for 1823: in that year there are 65 names of accountants, including those of such well-known men in their day as

Patrick Cockburn, John M'Kean (afterwards manager of the Scottish Widows' Fund), Claud Russell, Charles Selkrig, and William Paul (afterwards manager of the Commercial Bank). At that time accountants were few in number, and any one who thought himself fit could practise as such.

At first Mr Lindsay's progress was slow, but his business increased rapidly after his abilities and high character came to be known. What appears to have brought him into notice was his reports under remits from the Court. At that time accountants seem to have been given to producing reports of inordinate length, and I remember in my early professional life seeing one by a then well-known accountant, whom it would be invidious to name, which, after giving a prolix statement of the case, wound up with a progressive interest statement on fifty large folio pages! What information these details could have conveyed to the mind of a judge it is hard to say. Mr Lindsay set himself against such a practice, and his clear head and terse style of composition eminently fitted him for the task. He was a man of calm judgment and singularly judicial mind, and was well qualified to present knotty points of accounting to the Court in a brief and lucid shape: he took a powerful grasp of the essential points in a case, and brought a powerful judgment to bear upon them.

In those days commercial law was in somewhat of a chaotic state: it was before the Apportionment Act was held to apply to Scotland, and also the time when, to the horror of many, disentails became possible, and it was necessary to apply actuarial methods to such transactions. The business of an Edinburgh accountant was then very different from what it is now. Mr Lindsay had at that time the care of two or three large trusts and sequestrations, and was the adviser in the management of some great estates, and there was a continuous flow of remits from the Court, requiring in the accountant much knowledge of law and power of weighing evidence. Mr Lindsay never himself worked much at details, but he had a way of putting pertinent questions and examining results which very soon brought any error in detail to light. He would sit in his comfortable well-padded chair by the fire, having beside him the prints of a case on his little round table, and say to his partner, " I am going to the country and shall be back in a few days, and by that time you will be able to tell me whether the crux of the case does not rest on these points," and here he would present some jottings in pencil which he had made. Needless to say that the crux was where Mr Lindsay indicated. When he wrote anything himself he was very clear and concise, and not a word was added where unnecessary: it was alleged in his office that he wrote so concisely because he disliked the physical labour of writing, but the true reason, no doubt, was that he knew clearly what he wished to say.

Mr Lindsay was an ordinary director of the Royal Bank of Scotland with short intervals from 1843 to 1866, and afterwards an extraordinary director down to 1871.

In the year 1837 he was appointed auditor of the Scottish Widows' Fund Society, an office which he held for the long period of thirty years. An excerpt from the resolution of the directors at the close of his connection with the society in June 1867 may not be out of place :—

> When, in 1837, the late Mr Patrick Cockburn, accountant (who had been auditor from the commencement of the Society), died, and a successor fell to be appointed, Mr Lindsay's position and eminent qualifications pointed him out as peculiarly well fitted to supply Mr Cockburn's place. From the time of his appointment Mr Lindsay devoted his professional skill and unremitting attention to the business and affairs of the Society, and during the first years of his appointment especially, the labour and responsibilities devolving upon him in conjunction with the manager were very onerous, and the services which he then rendered were exceedingly valuable. . . . In accepting Mr Lindsay's resignation the directors desire to record the high sense which they, in common with all their predecessors in the direction, and indeed with all who are interested in the Society, have of the great value of the services rendered by Mr Lindsay.

Mr Lindsay was the senior partner of the firm of Lindsay, Jamieson, & Haldane.

Mr Lindsay was much liked by those who knew him well, and he had among men several very devoted friends, notably Mr John Mackenzie, who was manager of the Scottish

Widows' Fund during the greater part of the time that Mr Lindsay held the auditorship. In his earlier days he might have been seen with great good-humour playing " quadrille " with a party of old ladies who much appreciated his attention, while to the young he was throughout his life kind and bountiful. For a good many years previous to his retirement from business Mr Lindsay lived in the country, coming to Edinburgh for two or three days a-week; and in the year 1867 he finally retired from active life to Ardargie, a pretty country house in Perthshire on the May, opposite Invermay, where he and Mr Fotheringham continued their common housekeeping —keeping open house and dispensing kindly hospitality to their friends; and where Mr Lindsay interested himself much in looking after his farm and keeping its accounts, which, however, his friends suspected did not show a good balance, notwithstanding the skill and experience in accounting which were brought to bear upon them.

Mr Lindsay had little severe illness, and died suddenly and peacefully at an advanced age on the 17th of December 1876, when he had guests in the house, with whom he had been conversing cheerfully before he went to bed. He was a great reader, but his last few years were spent in partial blindness, when he would sit in his arm-chair knitting busily, to keep his hands employed while he enjoyed the company and took part in the conversation of his friends.

Mr Lindsay became a member of the Society of Accountants in Edinburgh at the time of its incorporation in the year 1854, and on looking over the list of original members one cannot but feel that the present position of the Society is, in some measure at least, due to the fact that many of its founders were men of the highest integrity and character, and among these we may fitly place Donald Lindsay.

JAMES HALDANE.

THE TREATMENT OF BAD AND DOUBTFUL DEBTS.

THE best method of dealing with bad and doubtful debts in the books of a commercial concern seems to be a matter that has received too little consideration. The prevalent practice appears to be simply to charge losses directly against revenue when they disclose themselves, and frequently no provision is made for unascertained losses. In businesses where credit for any lengthened period is given, it is obviously wrong to act on this principle, since the losses emerging in one year may to a great extent have really been incurred at some previous period. This is not balanced by the losses incurred but not ascertained during the year which is being dealt with, since the volume and conditions of business may have been very different in one period from those of another. For instance, a business which is rapidly expanding year by year, would exaggerate the amount of its apparent profits if it followed this system. Or take a concern which has been newly converted into a limited liability company, and has not taken over the risk of collection of the book debts. In the first year of its operations there would probably be very few bad debts which had been ascertained, yet if the company had been carrying on the same business as had been done formerly, there is no reason why the charge against revenue should be less than the average of previous years. A company in such a case is bound to provide out of revenue a reserve for bad and doubtful debts sufficient to cover the unascertained losses as nearly as they can be estimated. To do so is, indeed at all times, a duty of trading concerns giving credit if their balance-sheets are to show correctly the position of the business, but the example given above will show how also the amount of the year's profits may be over-stated if this is not kept in view.

If the amount of unascertained losses can be estimated with tolerable accuracy, then the amount of the losses which disclose themselves during the year—*plus* the estimate for unknown losses at the end of the year, and *minus* the corresponding estimate at the commencement—will represent the amount properly chargeable against the revenue of the year. In most public companies, however, as well as in many private concerns, it is desirable that an item which is necessarily so variable in amount should be averaged, so that the annual dividend should neither be unduly increased in a lucky year, nor unduly depressed in an unfortunate one. It is recognised that in part at least such results are due to chance, and should not be allowed to affect to their full extent the balance of profit to be divided.

Moreover, when it is considered how in nearly every business it is almost impossible to estimate the amount of unascertained losses with any degree of accuracy, it will be seen that a system of providing for bad debts based on average experiences is the best and most practicable.

In the case we have mentioned—that of a company acquiring a going business without taking the risk of collecting the book debts—the proper course would be first to ascertain what proportion the net losses by bad debts bore to the credit sales in the past experience of the business. A period of not less than five years would probably be necessary to give a fair average. The average rate per cent of losses having thus been ascertained, the amount which this produces when applied to the credit sales of the year in question should be debited to revenue and credited to a bad debt reserve account. This reserve account would be debited with the actual losses ascertained during the year, and the balance would be carried forward to the credit of the following year.

The same process would be followed each succeeding year, and if the business was carried on under normal conditions, the result would be that each year's revenue would be charged with a sum for bad debts bearing a fair relation to the actual amount placed at risk during that year, and there would always be at the credit of bad debt reserve a sum commensurate with the amount of accounts outstanding.

In businesses where customers receive cash advances as well as ordinary credit, and where, when a loss occurs, it may be impossible—as is usually the case—to distinguish satisfactorily between the loss on the cash account and that on the goods account, it may be found better to calculate the average loss by bad debts not as a percentage of the credit sales but of the amount due to the company in respect of goods and cash advances at the *commencement* of each of the years dealt with. This plan has also the advantage of automatically adapting itself to any general contraction or extension of credit which the company may have instituted. The method of taking the amount of credit sales for the year will probably, however, be preferred in most cases.

It might sometimes, no doubt, be necessary to alter the rate per cent assumed to represent average losses in the light of later experience, or to provide for altered conditions, but if the rate has been based on sufficient data no alteration should be made, in ordinary circumstances, except after the experience of a good many years. If it should unfortunately happen that losses are sustained which more than absorb the bad debt reserve, of course the balance must be provided from revenue; but after the first year or two, when there has been time to accumulate a fair amount of reserve, this is unlikely to occur, unless through reckless trading.

It may be urged as an objection to this system, that it tends to lessen that attention to the prevention of losses by bad debts which is given when the ascertained losses appear in the profit and loss account. The same objection, however, applies to any kind of reserve. A proper annual statement will show not only what has been charged against revenue, but also what has been done with all the reserves with which the year commenced; and the ordinary business man will have no difficulty in seeing, by the condition of the bad debt

The Treatment of Bad and Doubtful Debts.

reserve, whether his losses have been above or below the average.

In order to exercise an efficient oversight of debts which have become doubtful, the balance on the debtors' accounts should be transferred from the ordinary ledger to a bad debt ledger or register immediately the giving of further credit has ceased. The following is a form and ruling suggested for such a register, with examples of entries:—

[LEFT-HAND PAGE.]

Date of Transfer.	Page in Ledger.	Name.	Address.	Position of Debtor.
1896, May 10	247	James Ballantyne	Ormiston, East Lothian	Sequestrated 1st May 1896. (1)
1897, Jan. 3	373	David Ballingall	Merchant, Cupar-Fife	Signed Trust Deed 28th Dec. 1896. (2)
1897, Dec. 15	62	Andrew Baird	Grocer, Motherwell	Called meeting and offered composition 10th Dec. 1897. (3)
1897, Dec. 31	131	James Baxter	Ironmonger, Bo'ness	Acceptance for £100 dishonoured 20th Dec. 1897. (4)

[RIGHT-HAND PAGE.]

In hands of	Amount of debt.	Dividends, &c., received.		Written off for estimated loss.		Date when estate closed.	Remarks.
		Dates.	Amounts.	Dates.	Amount.		
(1) David Young, C.A., Trustee	£ s. d. 36 12 5	1896. Nov. 12 1897. Feb. 12	£ s. d. 6 2 1 1 0 4	1896. Dec. 31 1897. June 30	£ s. d. 25 0 0 4 10 0	1897. May 15	Bankrupt discharged Nov. 1896.
(2) Arthur Walker, Edinburgh, Trustee (claim with interest £99)	97 10 0	1897. April 5	49 10 0	1897. June 30 Dec. 31	40 0 0 8 0 0	1897. July 31	..
(3) Anderson & Wallace, Glasgow, Law Agents	132 0 0	1898. Jan. 15.	33 0 0	..	..	..	Composition Bills received due:— Jan. 15, '98, £33, July 15, '98, £33.
(4) Scottish Trade Protection Society	253 6 0	..	..	..	..	..	Summons served 31st Jan. 1898.

The book should be cut as an index throughout, and perhaps half-a-dozen lines allowed for each account. Where general ledger accounts are kept for each subsidiary ledger, there should be a bad debt ledger account, the balance of which would represent the sum of the balances appearing in the above book. The sums written off and credited in the accounts as above would be debited to the bad debt reserve account already referred to.

By keeping the bad and doubtful debts in a separate book in this manner, much closer attention can be given to the recovery of such sums as are possible, and there is less likelihood of a doubtful debt being overlooked until it is prescribed or has otherwise become absolutely irrecoverable.

The Accountants' Magazine.

Income tax. WHEN introducing the Budget in April last the Chancellor of the Exchequer intimated his desire that a committee should be appointed in connection with the income tax to inquire into "its incidence, the equity of its burdens, its machinery, and into the evasions." The suggestion was received with general approval, and a committee will no doubt be appointed before the end of the session.

There are probably no members of the community outside of the revenue officials who are so intimately acquainted with the practical operation of the Income Tax Acts as practising accountants. It has become the custom for business concerns to ask an accountant to prepare their returns of profits for assessment under Schedule D, which are often of a much more complex nature than people imagine. By doing so they usually save themselves, as well as the local surveyor, a troublesome correspondence in connection with explanations and particulars required, and in many cases they have saved money, because it is by no means an uncommon thing to find business men, through inadequate acquaintance with the intricacies of the tax, returning a larger sum for assessment than the amount liable to duty.

It is within the knowledge of all that of recent years the

income tax has been levied with much greater stringency than at one time prevailed, and to this is partly attributable the steadily-increasing yield per penny of the tax, to which the Chancellor of the Exchequer referred with satisfaction. No one can complain of the tax being fairly and strictly imposed, though the procedure of late has caused the just to suffer in many ways for the unjust; but it is to be feared that the revenue officials, in their desire that nothing should escape, have stretched their powers a little further than the law countenances. For instance, it has become the practice for the surveyors to request all companies and private business concerns of any importance to furnish in support of their return of profits a copy of their profit and loss account, and a statement showing how the amount of assessable profit is arrived at. Quite recently the surveyors have gone a step further, and have been requesting a copy of the accounts as soon as they are ready, and *before* the taxpayer's return is made, in a circular commencing " In order to the completion of the assessment under Schedule D." The basis of the assessment for income tax under Schedule D is a return to be made by the taxpayer. There is no power in the surveyor to require in any instance the production of accounts or statements of particulars, still less to complete the assessment from such accounts instead of from the taxpayer's return. Where he attempts to make up the assessment from the accounts he is more than likely to arrive at an erroneous result (and usually, though no doubt unintentionally, to the taxpayer's prejudice), since very few profit and loss accounts are made up in such a manner as to show the exact amount liable for income tax. It is true that the taxpayer can practically be compelled in the long run to produce his books and accounts, because the surveyor can impose such an assessment as will force him to take an appeal to the Commissioners against the amount, in which case he must produce his books to support his appeal. But this is a very different position from that assumed by the surveyors. Another matter in a very similar case is the return on form No. 46, now called for from all companies of the amount of all salaries, fees, wages, &c., paid to any officer employed by the company. This matter was dealt with in vol. i. of this Magazine, p. 349.

We do not quarrel with the request to furnish these particulars. No honest person objects to give the surveyors every reasonable facility for making a correct assessment. But we suggest that the law and the practice do not quite harmonise, and that it is not altogether a satisfactory state of matters under which the surveyors can only obtain one thing by threatening to do another which would be more disagreeable to the taxpayer.

It is perhaps inevitable in the collection of such a tax, but it is certainly unfortunate, that the relations between the surveyor and the taxpayer should so often be those of antagonism. For this the increasing and unauthorised demands of the revenue are partly responsible, but, besides, the surveyors do not always show that alacrity to point out to the taxpayer when he is making an over-payment which might engender a feeling of mutual confidence. No doubt also the usual attitude of the taxpayer is that of making the best bargain he can for himself. One remedy for this is that matters should be left more in the hands of independent men. The taxpayer has in numerous instances shown his readiness to leave the figures to the adjustment of a professional accountant; let the revenue officials place more reliance than they have been in the habit of doing on returns which have been so prepared. It is a little annoying to a man whose business it is to state accounts properly and who has been introduced into the matter for no other object but to ensure accuracy, to find his figures overhauled and questioned, and elementary and often absurd interrogations addressed to him as if he had any interest to defraud the revenue or had no knowledge of what he was doing. The Taxes Management Act enacts that no barrister or solicitor shall be allowed to plead before the Commissioners in an appeal. It is satisfactory to note that the Chancellor of the Exchequer considers it a hardship that a taxpayer should not have the assistance of a solicitor or an accountant in such circumstances. And we hope this may indicate a disposition to a fuller recognition in this connection of the professional accountant, who is capable of rendering much assistance to the revenue.

There are many defects in the Income Tax Acts which might be remedied, and all those who have any acquaintance with the subject will welcome the appointment of this proposed Committee of Inquiry. Mr Ritchie stated that it was forty-two years since any similar inquiry had been held, and during that time many new circumstances have arisen and unforeseen difficulties emerged. There has been much litigation on the subject. Insurance companies in particular have had many disputes with the revenue: an important decision of the House of Lords was reported in our last number. Shipowners have had a long and arduous fight with the Commissioners,—a paper by Mr James Cormack in our first volume, page 620, dealt with the questions raised. Many cases of hardship never come to public knowledge, and in others the law gives no remedy, such, for instance, as that of the person who buys a life annuity and has to pay income tax on the repayment of his capital.

It is most desirable that the fullest information should be placed before this committee on the points which Mr Ritchie indicated as the subject of inquiry. Probably our readers, as a class, are better able to furnish such information than any other body of men outside the Government offices. We invite all interested in the subject to communicate with us, and we shall take care that any suitable facts and ideas are transmitted to the proper quarter.

THE RELATION OF AUDITORS TO PUBLIC COMPANIES.

By NEIL J. D. KENNEDY, Professor of Law in the University of Aberdeen.

(*Address delivered to Aberdeen Chartered Accountants' Students' Society.*)

I DO not know that I would have accepted quite so readily the invitation with which the Society honoured me if I had known that the Chairman was to raise the expectations of the audience so high as he has done, as to the kind of lecture which I should deliver. I have taken, or been given, a very wide subject, and I can only endeavour to deal with it in very general outline, laying down some leading principles rather than attempting too many illustrations. A lawyer, like an accountant, is supposed to know a little of every subject, and in the course of my twenty years or more at the Bar I have had many opportunities of being coached by accountants, of examining and even cross-examining them, and appearing before them as arbiters, particularly with regard to cases arising out of the Joint-Stock Companies' Acts. To-night I am to endeavour, not to teach you any part of your business, not to give infallible rules, but to sketch the relations in which, according to the law, auditors at present stand to companies, specially the duties and liabilities which arise out of the office of auditor.

It is only in comparatively recent years that the profession of accountant has acquired full legal and public recognition, and separate status. I think the oldest Charter was granted about fifty years ago, and it is only lately that certain of our universities have founded Chairs in Accounting. I refer particularly to the Universities of London, Birmingham, and Liverpool. But, whether the full legal recognition has come soon or late, the profession itself is as old, and as necessary, as trade and commerce. The two oldest secular professions are, I think, surveyors of land and accountants in commerce. I remember having read some interesting discoveries regarding the operations of accountants in Babylon some four thousand years ago. I daresay you would laugh at their methods of accounting, for they kept their accounts on clay tablets; but it is not so long ago, almost within living memory, that our own exchequer kept its accounts by notches on a bundle of sticks. Thus, four thousand years ago, in Babylon and Egypt, even as at the present day, wherever there were or are large partnerships, shipping transactions, risky voyages, policies of a peculiar kind of insurance, the services were required of an expert who could distinguish between capital account and revenue account, between the expenditure that should be placed to the one and the expenditure that should be placed to the other, and who should define and guard the interests of all the parties concerned. As soon as such transactions arise, we find the necessity for an auditor beginning to be felt, and we see some foreshadowing of the method in which his duties should be performed.

In the earlier centuries of the Christian era we can trace most elaborate systems of accounting, principally in connection with public accounts. The Imperial Treasury required accountants to verify the payment of taxes and the disbursements of public money, and apportion them under their proper heads, and to report to some authority. So the accountant in one of his most important functions got the name of auditor, for he examined the accounts, he heard the parties, and acted in a kind of judicial capacity. The employment of the auditor, of course, extended to the affairs of private life. Some Romans kept private auditors, and required an audit, up to date, at their dinner-parties, for the benefit of their guests. Whenever civilisation reaches the stage at which there are persons who administer, under a trust or agency, the property of other people, it is soon found that the aid of an expert is required to see that the beneficiaries get justice from the trustees who are managing their affairs. In this connection one fact, which we shall see abundantly illustrated in the examples which I shall lay before you, is that the ingenuity of persons who are managing other people's affairs, particularly when they desire to get a private advantage for themselves, is always a little in front of the ingenuity even of the best accountant in detecting it. The best policeman is never quite as clever as the most ingenious thief, and the law never provides quite sufficient means for effectually detecting the latest and most ingenious ways of committing the oldest kinds of fraud. Let us just take two characters out of that wellknown and most animated of all pictures of early England, Chaucer's 'Canterbury Pilgrimage.' Of one of the pilgrims it is recorded that he had been a sheriff and an accountant. But there is another character brought in, the reeve or factor of Norwich, whose character is very sharply drawn. It is said that he was richer than his lord, that he could lend to his lord his lord's own money, and get not only high interest but thanks for it. That is a most familiar form of fraud in later days. And then Chaucer says first, there was "no man who could bring him into arrearage,"— that is, no man could find out that he owed anything to his lord; and secondly, which is the more pertinent to this lecture, he says, "No auditor could on him win." Apparently many auditors had tried, but they had failed to protect the lord against the reeve.

There are two standards of liability arising out of employment, which are set up by the law. I do not speak of liability arising out of deliberate fraud, because everyone who defrauds, whether he is an expert or not, is liable in damages for the result to those who are injured by it; but I confine myself to liability arising from, or imposed by law in consequence of, employment. Now the two standards differ largely. In the first place, there is the liability of the ordinary person; but that is measured by the care and diligence which an ordinary person would give to the particular matter in hand. We don't require from the ordinary man the skill and care of the expert. Thus it is not expected of the ordinary director that he should have the skill of an expert valuator or an expert accountant. He is entitled to rely on what he believes to be an honest and fair representation of experts, because he is not expected to possess such knowledge, although he may find that he has made himself liable by professing it and meddling with what he knows nothing about. The other standard of liability is entirely different, in the sense that it is a much higher and more exacting one,—the standard of duty required by law from the person who holds himself out as an expert in the particular matter for which he is employed. He must devote to his duties the reasonable care and skill which a man fairly well versed in his profession would give to the matter; or, in other words, he is expected to follow, and as a general rule is safe to follow, the usual practice of his profession. If he deviates too far from it, he does so at his peril, and may thereby incur liability for neglect of proper care and skill, which arises from the fact of his employment and the fact of his having an expert knowledge, and which may be enforced by any one towards whom the duty of taking proper care and skill exists. The liability of an expert may, however, arise in another or an additional way. Suppose he gets, either from an Act of Parliament or from a person employing him, instructions to proceed on particular lines, to show certain results of accounts, to distinguish different departments of accounts, then it is his duty to follow these instructions, assuming them to be lawful, and any material deviation from them is a failure in specific duty, for which, if damage results, he will be liable to any person who employed him, and has suffered by that failure in duty.

Particularly in the relation of auditors to public companies, these two grounds of the liability of an expert do not necessarily coincide. They have to be taken together; that is to say, in so far as there are not express instructions either by statute or the constitution of the company as to the particular matter, the expert must follow the usual practice of his profession, and a departure from it may expose him to the liability I have mentioned. Of course, he is not liable for mere errors in judgment, though an error in judgment may be so great as to be evidence of ignorance, nor is he liable for taking one opinion prevalent in his profession rather than another which also may have much support, or even be the opinion of the majority. In short, as far as the standard of his general expert capacity is concerned, he is not liable unless he has acted so as to show ignorance of his business or serious negligence.

Now let me give some examples of distinctions which are quite recognised in themselves, but upon the application of which opinions might very well differ, and where there would be neither negligence nor ignorance shown in taking one side or the other. There is no distinction more fixed or more important in itself than the distinction between capital account and revenue account, and yet opinions may largely differ as to whether certain items of expenditure should be placed to capital or should come out of revenue—for example, the kind of expenditure which is not merely the renewing of fixed assets so as to maintain them, but includes also the cost of additional assets or permanent machinery used as assets. Let us take another example. Fixed capital is, generally speaking, that which is not intended to be consumed, or, if from its nature it must be consumed, is intended to be continuously replaced, and which is the permanent means of a company earning profits, and consists of visible, tangible assets. On the other hand, floating capital consists of assets which more or less perish in the using. The purpose of having them is that they should perish or be transformed, and that thereby profits should be earned. But it may be a very difficult matter sometimes to say whether given subjects should be regarded as fixed capital or floating capital. The practical importance of this distinction is very great, because if what is floating capital is lost, then such loss must be replaced, in the ordinary case, before the profits can be ascertained; and if the loss swallows up the profits, then there are no profits out of which a dividend can be declared. For instance, suppose the business of a company is dealing in shares of other companies, the shares which that company buys and sells are part of its ordinary stock-in-trade, and are therefore floating capital. Any loss upon transactions in these shares should be charged to revenue and taken into account before a dividend can be declared. I remember two eminent accountants being divided in opinion as to whether the horses of a tramway company, which was about to change its system of haulage from horse to cable, were floating capital or not. In a case of that kind a man would not be liable if he took either side, because on either side there is a reasonable amount of opinion.

Another subject on which many experts differ in opinion is the manner in which the depreciation of fixed assets should be dealt with. That you must allow for such depreciation in some way is, of course, the principle; but you find experts advocating different methods in the same case, and it may depend on circumstances whether one method or another is the more convenient. We may, for instance, charge to revenue the exact cost of maintenance and a fraction of the original cost, so that when the asset comes to be realised it may stand in the books at not more than its true value. On another theory (and I have heard some accountants say in the box that it is the best, theoretically at least), the asset is first entered at its original cost; a valuation is made by an expert every year, or at fixed periods, and the asset is written down from year to year, or, it may be, written up, according to the amount of the valuation. There are, of course, other methods, such as creating reserve funds, sinking funds, &c. In fact, there are five or six methods, some more appropriate to certain companies than to others, according to certain kinds of assets—*e.g.*, wasting assets and reversions; but they are all legitimate methods for bringing about the same result. Let me take another example. I think many accountants differ as to what is the proper meaning of the words "reserve fund" in a balance-sheet. Many hold that a reserve fund means nothing more than the amount of profits divisible, but not actually divided, and therefore that you may call the profits which you have not divided a reserve fund, whatever may be the form in which they happen to be at the moment of issuing the balance-sheet. On the other hand, the strictest accountants think that the term "reserve fund" should be confined to the case where profits divisible but not divided have been invested in some form, or appropriated to some specific purpose such as the equalisation of subsequent dividends, or meeting bad debts, or depreciation, unexpected losses, or the like. That, again, is a matter of opinion; the practical point is that in a balance-sheet what is meant by reserve, or suspense fund, should be stated or apparent. So there are many open questions: for example, where a company issues new shares at a premium, are these premiums divisible as profits, or should they be carried to capital receipts? I think the latter is the sounder course.

As there is no form of commercial association which creates so many opportunities for fraud as the joint-stock company, so there is no class of cases in which Parliament from time to time has more anxiously endeavoured to provide securities against fraud and misappropriation. I may just in passing say that I think that some bankers, solicitors, and accountants are not sufficiently careful to see that their names do not appear on the outside of prospectuses. That is not enough to make them liable for what the prospectus contains, but it is a fact which may go a long way towards showing that they authorised the statements made in the prospectus; and therefore in general, unless one is very certain of the prospectus and of the company, it is not wise to do an act which may give colour to other acts, and in the end lead to liability.

Joint-stock companies are just large partnerships, with some differences; principally, so far as we at present are concerned, that the great majority of the members or shareholders are just sleeping partners, the right of management being confided to a body of directors, who are usually appointed by the constitution of the company originally framed, but subsequently elected by the shareholders. There are three things about a company which, from the legal point of view, one must always keep in mind. The first is, that no company can legally pay dividends out of capital: of course some do, as practice does not always correspond with theory. In the second place, no company can issue shares at a discount, although that has been attempted. In the third place, no company can engage in business or borrow money outside its powers: to ascertain the extent of these powers, one must look at the memorandum and articles of association, which are its constitution, and the Acts of Parliament by which the Company is regulated.

There are other practical features about a company which have also an important bearing on auditors and their functions. Shareholders, taken as a whole, are often an ignorant (though there are individuals of a suspecting mind), a trusting, and always a very inert body. They require protection; to give it is the object of the appointment of an auditor. The managing director or the secretary (sometimes the two offices are combined) may find that by the constitution of the company his salary or fees are dependent upon apparent profits; and he sometimes, perhaps not altogether without intention, fixes the fee of the auditor at as low a figure as possible. I do not think it is always to save fees. The result is apparent, and I do not say that it is altogether an unexpected result, for a man is very apt to measure the amount of work he has to do by the fee he is to get for it. If he gets a fee corresponding to one day's personal work he is not inclined to give a fortnight's work. Now that is not only a matter for the auditor but for the shareholders. The shareholders ought to realise that the auditor is appointed for their protection, and therefore when they elect an auditor they should take a sufficient interest to see that the auditor gets a fair remuneration. I have known a very large company fix the fee of the auditor at five guineas, while a careful audit would have taken an accountant and his staff four or five days. Of course I do not say every man yields, but there is always a temptation to do little and general work instead of much and particular work, when the fee is clearly inadequate.

Companies have another feature, a very practical feature, which distinguishes them from a private partnership: their officials feel that there is a pressing necessity for having a dividend every year. In a private concern, if a man finds he has not made profits nobody need be the wiser; but in a company, if there is no dividend, its creditors may make a run upon it, and the value of its shares may be enormously depressed, although the company may be a sound enough concern. The private trader can wait till the clouds roll by; the officials of the company feel bound to deny that there are any clouds in their financial sky. The reason why I am pointing out this risk is this: every year, in some company or another, a managing director, or it may be the leading officials, without any fixed intention of being dishonest and without needing to cover anything of the nature of defalcation, feel that there is a sort of higher duty, or a stronger faith in the future, which compels them to amend the balance-sheet so as to make profits appear where no profits have been actually earned. That is just where the auditor comes in as a check on the vivid imagination or sanguine temperament, and as a protection to the shareholders. There have also been many cases in which the chairmen of companies, directors, and others have deliberately falsified accounts to conceal the fact that they had taken loans to themselves from the company and had quite forgotten the necessity of paying them back. But the methods of altering the balance-sheet are often very much alike, whether the purpose of alteration is to conceal personal dishonesty, misappropriation, or defalcation, or whether it is done, which they may not think dishonest, to conceal the fact that there have been very serious losses on the year's transactions of the company. It is often done by an over-valuation of assets, or over-statement of profits, but more often by an under-statement of liabilities. In any or all of these ways, one can succeed in preparing an apparently satisfactory balance-sheet, when the real state of matters is far from being rosy,—a sort of "primrose path" to ruin.

The duties of the auditor of a public company involve, in the first place, the use of reasonable skill and care on his part as an expert; and secondly, obedience to all statutory instructions which affect audit, given with relation to companies in general. If, as in some cases, there is a special Act, or special clauses in the constitution of the company, he must study the special points in regard to which he is to apply his skill and care. He must always remember that he is put in office to guard the interests of the shareholders. He is a servant of the shareholders, or rather, he holds a kind of judicial position between the shareholders and the directors. In a certain sense he may be called the servant of the directors, but he really represents the shareholders against the permanent staff and the directors. Thus he may be subject to a much greater liability than a director for the balance-sheet and accounts. A director may say, "I honestly, not knowing that anything was wrong, accepted this report on the certificate of the auditor;" and if he did so honestly, without any reasonable ground of suspicion, the director would escape liability, where the auditor might be found liable. The duties of the auditor begin when the accounts are made up and delivered to him. I think (leaving out of view certain corporations and cases under special Acts of Parliament) that the employment of an independent auditor was first made imperative by public statute in the case of railway companies. In the Railway Act of 1867 (30 & 31 Vict. c. 126, sect. 30) there are explicit directions laid down with regard to the examination of the books and the accounts. No dividend can be paid until the auditors have certified that the accounts are accurate and the dividend earned; and the auditors are empowered to issue to the shareholders independently any statement regarding the financial position and prospects of the company which they may think material for the information of the shareholders. Audit was next made imperative by public statute by the Act of 1879, in the case of banks, which became joint stock companies after the year 1879. That was directly in consequence of the revelations about the finances of the City of Glasgow Bank: prior to the Act of 1879 there was no law making it compulsory for banks to appoint auditors. As regards joint-stock companies, the Companies Act of 1862 provided a model set of articles or regulations known as "Table A." These articles were binding on every company which adopted them, but companies were free to leave them out of their constitution, or to alter them, with exceptions immaterial to our purpose. That was a blot on the Act of 1862. Among these articles we find provisions inadequate, because only permissive (articles 83-94 inclusive), as to the election and duties of an independent auditor for the protection of shareholders.

Well, even Parliament can see a blot after it has been pointed out, and in 1900 a new Act, 63 & 64 Vict. c. 48, was passed to make audit compulsory. Sections 21 to 23 inclusive lay down the minimum regulations with regard to the auditor: no company can take away from these, though it may, of course, impose additional precautions. It is provided that an auditor is to be appointed by the company at each annual general meeting, to hold office for a year. If no appointment is made, any member of the company may apply to the Board of Trade to appoint an independent auditor, and that is a very good way of ensuring that an auditor is appointed by the company. The auditor must not be a director or an officer of the company. There is no law against his being a shareholder,—some of the older Railways Acts required that he should,—it is not material whether he is or not. The remuneration of the auditor has to be fixed by the company, in general meeting. Then come the powers of the auditor, which are conferred upon him in virtue of his judicial position, as I said, between the shareholders and the directors. He has a right of access at all times to the books and accounts. He is entitled to require from the directors and officers of the company any information and explanation necessary for the performance of his duties. With regard to his duties, he must sign a certificate, at the foot of the balance-sheet, stating whether his requirements as auditor have been complied with, and he must make a report to the shareholders on the accounts examined and on every balance-sheet laid before the company in general meeting; and in his report he must state whether the balance-sheet exhibits a true and correct view of the state of the company's affairs as shown by the books of the company. These are the minimum powers and the minimum duties which the Act of 1900 lays down. The auditor must satisfy himself as to whether the company has any special or additional regulations of its own, and also how far "Table A" has been adopted, and thereby binds the company. I mean the articles 83 to 94 inclusive, so far as different from but not contradictory of these enactments of the Act of 1900. As regards appointment and remuneration of auditors, and the necessity for an audit of accounts and balance-sheets at least once every year, "Table A" agrees with the Act of 1900; but there are some important points in "Table A" which do not occur in the Act of 1900, and therefore would not affect a company which is governed, as to this, only by the Act of 1900—namely, that (1) every auditor shall have a list delivered to him of all books kept by the company; and (2) he may, at the expense of the company, employ accountants to assist him; and while he may require information from the directors and officers of the company, under the Act of 1900, he may (3), in connection with the accounts, examine the directors or any other officers of the company.

The only other matter I have to refer to before giving some practical examples is that an auditor appointed or elected by a company is a regular officer of the company, and accordingly is liable to the summary remedies provided by the Act of 1862 against officers of a company. These are much quicker than the ordinary remedies, particularly the remedy given by section 165, though this remedy only arises when the natural result of bad management is reached, and the company goes into liquidation. The liquidator (*i.e.*, the legal representative of the company—for the purpose of winding up) is entitled in summary process to ask the Court to assess damages against any director, manager, or any officer of such company, where that officer has been guilty of any breach of trust in relation to the company, and he may compel such director, manager, or officer to repay any money so applied or retained together with interest by way of compensation. I should say, to be accurate, that this section applies now only to Scotland, having been superseded by a similar provision in the English Act of 1890, 53 and 54 Vict. c. 63, sect. 10, so far as England is concerned.

Some auditors have rather thought that it was their duty merely to see that the additions are correct, and that the balance-sheet corresponds with the balances shown by books of the company, that they may shut their eyes to any suspicious items, or items requiring investigation or further information. You will see that they run great risks by taking such narrow views. Most of the cases where they have suffered for their neglect have come into Court in England, few in Scotland. Take, for instance, Leeds Estate Building and Investment Company, Limited, in 1887, L.R. Ch.D. 787. The manager and the auditor of that company were held liable jointly and severally to repay in full the sums distributed by the company during the years 1878-1879 as dividends, because in point of fact these had never been earned but had been paid out of capital. Indeed the company from its incorporation earned no profits, but every year its balance-sheet showed profits, and a dividend was paid which varied from $2\frac{1}{2}$ per cent up to 10 per cent. The manager was certainly dishonest, but the auditor was not; he was just careless, or thought that the directors would think more of him if he did not criticise their proceedings. In this case, the manager, after he had made up a draft balance-sheet, proceeded to calculate how much dividend would be expected that year, and then increased the amount of loans to customers, and anticipated interest not yet payable to an amount sufficient to make it appear that the required dividend was being paid out of the year's profits. He also did what should certainly have awakened the suspicions of the auditor. Without any certificates of an expert, or any reason except that of making the balance-sheet look well, he, by a stroke of his pen, increased nearly threefold the value of the offices in which the bank conducted its business. One year the office furniture was valued at £15; and I should suppose that by the next year it had rather depreciated than otherwise, but instead of appearing at the same or a reduced value, it figured in the balance-sheet at the value of £150. This increase would have appeared on comparison. Whether the auditor could have discovered the overstatement of loans as easily is not quite so clear. Now the auditor certified that the balance-sheets were true copies of those shown in the books of the company. A certificate of that kind was very ambiguous. The balance-sheets were true copies of the balance-sheets shown in the books; but I should think that the ordinary shareholder would read his certificate in another way—namely, that the balance-sheets were true copies of the balances brought out by the books. Accordingly the auditor was held liable to repay the dividends which had been paid out of capital.

Now, let me take another example, where the auditor was not found liable, but where the case was such a narrow one that the judge of first instance, Lord Justice Vaughan, probably the English judge most experienced in commercial and bankruptcy law, held the auditor liable (but the Appeal Court held that the auditor was not liable) for a particular error in the balance-sheet. This case was the Kingston Cotton Mill Company in 1896, L.R. 1 Ch. 331 and 2 Ch. 279, and arose like the example just quoted, after the company had gone into liquidation. Balance-sheets for several successive years, always showing a profit, were signed by the auditor; but that profit had been made to appear by overstating, as far as was necessary, (1) the value of the machinery, &c., allowing little or nothing for depreciation; and (2) the amount and the value of the stock-in-trade. Of course, if you choose to say falsely that you have £20,000 of goods ready to be sent out when you have only £10,000, you can construct a highly satisfactory balance-sheet. Now, if both these overstatements were set right, there were no profits earned at all; but it required both of them to bring matters to the point of proof that the company had really earned no profits. The manager was, quite rightly, I think, held liable to repay the dividend which had been paid. Lord Justice Vaughan decided that the auditor was also liable, because, though he had not discovered the overstatement of the amount of the stock-in-trade, there were various other things which should have made him suspect, and, having made him suspect, should have made him investigate. There was no doubt that the auditor was an honest man, and was not intending to shield the manager or anybody else. It was quite true that if the auditor had taken the stock-book, and then gone round the actual stock and ticked off the particular bales and boxes, he would have found out that there was an overstatement. Lord Justice Vaughan held that he should have done so; but I think you will probably agree that the Appeal Court took a sounder view when they said that, as there were no circumstances to awaken strong suspicion, it was no business of an auditor personally to take stock, when he had before him the stock-book and a certificate by the manager that it was correct. Accordingly, the Appeal Court held that the only charge which could be brought against the auditor was that he failed to detect the manager, and that was insufficient to make him liable, because he had no reason to believe that the manager was dishonest. This is one of the best examples of circumstances in which the auditor just escaped liability.

Let me take two examples from banking companies—the one where the auditor was held liable, and the other the well-known case of the City of Glasgow Bank, in which, if there had been an independent auditor, he would probably have discovered the falsehoods in the balance-sheets, or prevented their being perpetrated, and so have saved the shareholders. Now, with regard to the first of these examples — namely, the London & General Bank in 1895, L.R. 2 Ch. 166 and 673, that was a bank which had been incorporated under the Act of 1879, and regulations substantially adopted from "Table A" were binding upon the officers and upon the auditors. The auditor was elected annually, and every balance-sheet had to be signed by the auditor. One is rather sorry for the auditor, because he was a man not dishonest, and easily influenced. However, he was held liable to repay the whole dividend for 1891, amounting to £8100. He did see that there was something not right, but he forgot that he was not the servant of the directors but the servant of the shareholders, and that it was not enough merely to communicate with the directors regarding matters which he should have reported to the shareholders. The London & General Bank, manager Mr Jabez Balfour, was supposed to do ordinary banking business, but was really a bank got up to find money for Jabez Balfour's other companies, which all were very good customers in the way of borrowing money. The balance-sheet of 1891, signed by the auditor, and for which the auditor was found liable, showed under the heading "Loans to Customers and other Securities" a total of £346,975. The auditor looking at that sum, and finding what it represented, was struck with the fact that the only security for any part of it was of the most shaky and contingent description, and accordingly he put in his report, which was laid before the directors and which he intended should be circulated among the shareholders, the words "values dependent on realisation," adding, "On this point I have reported specially to the Board." He did point out to the Board of Directors that that was a grossly exaggerated item. However, Mr Jabez Balfour got round him and induced him to strike out the statement that he had reported specially to the Board, and accordingly the report, as it went to the shareholders, read simply "Loans to Customers and other Securities, £346,975—values dependent on realisation." I suppose the value of securities is always dependent on realisation; so the statement might mean a little or it might mean a great deal. If he had given the warning to the shareholders that he gave to the directors, I think he might have just escaped liability.

The other case is that of the City of Glasgow Bank. As that bank was formed before the Act of 1879, it had no independent auditor. Observe how the fraud was effected. The balances in the balance-sheet were the same as the balances in the books, but the component items on each side were altered in order to conceal the losses arising out of illegitimate transactions. The managing director and some, at least, of the other directors proceeded in the following manner. Their bank accountant prepared a draft balance-sheet showing correctly what was in the books. Then the managing director and some of the other directors set to work to transform that draft into a fancy balance-sheet that would give an impression that the bank was highly prosperous. Remember what induced them to do this. They had lent nearly three millions (that is to say, three-fifths of their whole lending capital), principally to directors and their friends. Of course they charged interest on these loans, but they never got it. When they made a demand for interest some of the gentlemen to whom they had lent the money just said, "Lend us a little more or we cannot pay the interest; put it down somewhere in a book." And there was an interest book kept which the ordinary clerks were not allowed to see, showing some details of these operations. If an auditor had compared this balance-sheet with the books, he would have seen at once that the two did not agree. These directors, in making up the balance-sheet for a critical year, understated their deposit account by £440,738, and reduced their foreign credits by £1,400,000. (Now the purpose in making the changes was to bring out a dividend of 7 per cent for that particular year.) Then there was £680,000 due on credit account by some of those friends of theirs. These sums due by persons who, instead of being able to pay, could only borrow more, were entered in the balance-sheet partly as "cash in hand, gold, and notes," partly as "Government stock, exchequer bills, and other stock and debentures." There were securities of a kind held against some of these loans, and one of the bank officials when asked in court how he had valued them said, "Oh, I was told to value the securities just to make the account square."

I have not time to quote other later illustrative cases—which I had noted; so, in conclusion, I will sum up what I think are the most important points to be remembered. (1) The auditor holds office in the interests of the shareholders. (2) He is bound to make himself acquainted with the statutes and the memorandum and articles of association of the company. (3) He must also fulfil the requirements of any special regulations of the company as to audit. (4) He is bound to see that the accounts accurately represent the business done by the company; it is not enough that the accounts correspond with the books. (5) He must give the shareholders, and not merely the directors, information as to serious error, and still more as to fraud, or even grave irregularities where a satisfactory explanation has not been given. (6) He must certify nothing which he has not reasonable grounds for believing to be true. On a question of valuation, about which he is not supposed to be an expert, he is quite entitled to rely on a valuation made by a person reputed to be an expert in the particular matter; but on doubtful points it is his duty to ask explanations, if necessary, from the directors and other officers of the company, or, where he has the power, to examine them, to satisfy himself. He is not bound to suspect. In a case bearing on the point one of the judges said, "The auditor is a watch-dog for the shareholders, but he is not a bloodhound." This figure was intended to point out that, unless something occurs to awaken suspicion, he is not to assume that the manager, or the managing director, or the officials are endeavouring to commit an act of dishonesty. But, if he does see reason to suspect, he is bound to follow that up, and if the explanations are not satisfactory, then he must give sufficient information to the shareholders in his report to enable them to take action. An auditor requires, not merely the accountant's skill, but a considerable amount of judgment and common-sense, and the man who combines and applies these qualities will not find his reputation endangered or his pocket mulcted in damages by a court of law. Lawyers meet accountants in many ways — as judicial factors, as trustees in bankruptcy, as liquidators, as judicial referees—but I do not think that any of these offices require such a union of skill and tactful common-sense as the position, inadequately paid as it is, of auditor of a joint-stock company.

COST ACCOUNTS.

By FREDERICK TOD, C.A.

(A Lecture delivered before the Edinburgh Chartered Accountants' Students' Society on 23rd February 1905.)

IT will be advisable, before considering the practical working of cost accounts, to refer to the various reasons which makes the subject one of great importance and interest to accountants and to business men generally.

I. *Field for Specialisation.*—The prevailing and characteristic feature in present-day business and manufacturing, and also in professional life, is that of specialisation. With the advance of economic principles and practices, and in particular, the ever-growing tendency to further division of labour, there has arisen the need for men specially trained in, and conversant with, particular subjects. Accountants are defined as "those who are skilled in accounts," but the time is coming when members of the profession will need to take up a special branch of the profession and practice in it. Accounting is a wide field, and there are many parts of it in which they can specialise. Company management, bankruptcy, secretarial work, burgh and parochial audits, and commercial and industrial businesses as far as accounting is concerned therein. In the last class especially, the subject of costing offers such a field for special study, since it is as yet only at its beginning, and it is more and more being developed as men of business begin to realise its importance. In America this subject is receiving very great attention, the work of accountants there being chiefly in connection therewith.

II. *Help in Auditing.*—As auditors also, it is most important that accountants should be conversant with the subject. An auditor submits a profit and loss account to his client, shows him what the result of his year's trading has been, and how he stands financially. Then he may assume his work to be done. It is not necessarily so. His client may not understand how the result of the year's trading is so and so. Then is the time for an auditor well versed in costing to get his client to introduce such a system as will show him not only whether he has made a profit or loss, but how he has made it, and when and where. The distinction between cost accounts and a profit and loss account is well explained by Mr Mann, in his article on this subject in the 'Encyclopædia of Accounting': "Cost accounts are an analysis, a separating of details and particulars of costs; while, on the other hand, an ordinary profit and loss account or a trading account is a synthesis, a grouping together of results."

III. *Verifying Stock.*—In enabling us to verify the stock on hand, also, they are of assistance, as from the cost books we can get the cost of manufacture of the finished product, and see that they are in at their proper value in the stock sheets; and the balance in the stores accounts, as will be shown later, should equal the stores of material on hand, allowing for loss in manufacture and ordinary wastage.

IV. *Check on Work in Progress.*—Cost accounts are further of very great use in enabling an auditor to check the work in progress, as from the cost book he can extract the wages paid and material used in connection with the different jobs uncompleted at the date of closing the books.

V. *Flotation and Consolidation of Businesses.*—In connection, too, with the flotation and consolidation of businesses, it is indispensable for accountants to know the subject. In order to show the importance of costing in this connection, it may be pointed out that Mr G. A. Touch of London, who lectured to us last year on the subject of flotation and consolidation of businesses, gave the first place in his address to the importance of a study of the cost system. He says, speaking of the importance of this subject: "Where the business is of a complicated nature—and this chiefly applies to manufacturing concerns—it will be necessary for the accountant to make an examination of the system of cost accounts in use. It will be his duty to acquaint himself thoroughly with the working of the system, and, before going into details, to form an opinion as to whether it is theoretically sound and likely to accomplish the object in view. This is a point requiring particularly careful study in such trades as engineering, contracting, &c., because, owing to the large contracts which are undertaken nowadays, it is especially important to ascertain that a true apportionment of the cost is charged to each work." Mr Touch also lays particular stress on the importance of studying the cost records in connection with the examination of uncompleted contracts.[1]

Accountants, then, ought to lose no opportunities of insisting on the advantages of cost accounting, and of trying to persuade business people, who have not already adopted some system of cost accounts, to do so. The advantages to them are obvious. Firstly, they enable, as already stated, profits and losses to be localised. A business man can see what contracts pay and what do not. Secondly, they are of value to him in fixing his selling price of articles manufactured. Many a manufacturer has before now sold articles at what he thought to be remunerative prices, whereas if he had had accurate records of the cost of their manufacture kept, he would either have ceased to deal in those articles, or else have raised their selling price. It is, however, in estimating —*i.e.*, tendering for contracts—that cost accounts are so important to business men. Estimates are asked for a job.

[1] 'Accountants' Magazine,' 1904, pp. 256-259.

A manufacturer who has done similar work before and kept records of the cost thereof, turns up these records, and on their results bases his present estimate, allowing for change in market price of material and change in the rate of wages. He can compete with much more assurance than another who has not kept such records, and does not know whether his previous similar contracts have paid or not. Further, competition now is so keen and prices are cut so fine that it is imperative that manufacturers should in all ways be able to save expenses and run their businesses as economically as is possible, consistent with sound business principles; and if a man is to do so he must know where his money goes and find out where there is extravagance, and through a system of cost accounts he will be enabled to do so.

Such being the importance to accountants of making ourselves expert in costing, let us proceed to discuss it more closely. One of the first questions that naturally arises is, How far should a system of cost accounts fit in with the commercial accounts, and form part of the whole accounting system in a factory or business? This to a great extent depends on the nature of the business, and on what the cost accounts are intended to show. In some businesses it may be impossible or undesirable to make the costing as complete as in others. Where it is possible, however,—and it is in most cases,—the system should be so framed that the cost accounts can be balanced with the cash system; that the total wages paid and material used on contracts, &c., during the year, as shown by the cash system, have their counterpart analysis in the cost books with which they are reconciled. Of course, it is not necessary that the cost accounts should be mixed with the commercial accounts; rather the reverse—kept separate, the one being the complement of the other. It is evident, of course, that in certain businesses the commercial accounts *are* the cost accounts, as in a business which makes only one article of a certain size. Then to get the cost per unit, it is only necessary to take the total material used, wages, and all expenses, and divide the total of these by the number of the articles made during the year. Very few businesses are of this kind, however, and hence the necessity for a separate system of costing.

What, then, is it that we want a cost account to show? As the name implies, the cost of manufacture of an article. As regards things purchased for resale, cost in reference to these is the price paid for material, wages, oncost—that is, indirect expenses—and profit to the seller, or, in other words, the purchase price. But in regard to articles a manufacturer makes, the term has a different meaning. An illustration will explain this. A sculptor wants a bust of a certain person: two courses are open to him—he may either make one himself, or he may purchase one finished. In the latter case, the cost at which he will value it will be the maker's charge for material, labour, expenses, and profit. If he adopts the former plan, a different valuation will ensue. How is he then to arrive at the cost of the busts he himself carves, and the cost of other jobs and contracts he undertakes? By keeping a record of the material used on each piece of work, the wages paid in connection therewith, and all direct expenses, and adding a percentage for oncost. Let us consider, then, the various elements comprised in "cost," taking the above case. The first of these elements is that of materials. *Materials* will probably consist of at least two kinds—(1) materials ordered in connection with individual jobs which may be charged against these works direct; and (2) material which will go into store and be issued as occasion arises. It is advantageous, however, for all material, whether for special work or not, to be put into store and thence reissued, so that the stores books may be balanced with the commercial books at any time. Assuming the goods to have been ordered under proper authority, when they arrive they are checked as regards quantity and quality, and the invoices are checked for prices. The invoices should then be entered in the "stores received" book, which, in addition to the usual ruling *re* date, names, &c., should also contain columns for quantity as well as money value. From this they will be posted to the stores ledger Dr. side, under headings referring to the various kinds of material. The stores ledger should also be so ruled as to show quantity as well as money value. The invoices, after being entered in the stores received book, are sent to the invoice clerk, who enters them in detail in his invoice dissection book, crediting the various parties from whom the goods were got, and debiting the monthly total to a stores account in the general ledger. It will be seen at once that the total posted to the debit of stores account in the general ledger must agree with the aggregate total of the items posted to the different accounts in the stores ledger. In this connection it should be pointed out that a distinction is here made between stores and stock. By stock is meant the finished articles, and by stores is meant that from which the finished articles are made. As regards stores issued for jobs, the orders for those are given by the proper persons to the storekeeper, who enters them in his "stores issued" book, from which they are posted to the credit of the different accounts in the stores ledger, both as regards quantity and value. The total of the stores issued book for each fortnight or month is posted to the credit of the stores account in the general ledger, and to the debit of a cost ledger account in the general ledger. An allocation is also made for the same periods of the stores issued book, showing for what works the various stores were issued, and the detailed totals of this allocation sheet are posted to the debit of accounts for the various jobs in a cost ledger. The cost ledger contains an account for each contract or job, such account being debited with all items of cost applicable thereto and its proportion of oncost, and credited with tender price and extras added, the balance on the account being the profit or loss,—profit if a credit balance and loss if a debit balance. It will be evident that if it is desired to get the value of the stores on hand, all one has to do is to take the balance of the stores account in the general ledger, and if it is desired to know how much of a particular material is on hand, by turning up that article in the stores ledger one will get both the quantity and value of that particular store on hand; and thus the storekeeper can always see that his stores are being kept up to any required minimum. The aggregate balances of the stores ledger must of course agree with the balance in the stores ledger account in the general ledger.

After material comes *Labour*. Means are taken to record the daily time worked by each man on the different jobs. This is done in different ways, by pass-books, sheets, or otherwise. An allocation is made, say, each fortnight, showing the total hours expended by each man, and the wages earned, and also showing the works in respect of which the wages are paid. The total wages paid is posted to the wages account in the general ledger, and the amount of this which is in payment of work on contracts is transferred from here to the debt of the cost ledger account in the general ledger. The details of the amount thus transferred are posted from the wages allocation sheet to the different jobs in the cost ledger. The balance in the wages account in the general ledger represents labour expended not directly on specific jobs, but on general work, as cleaning up the works, &c., goes to form part of the oncost. Thus it is seen that wages are quite capable of being reconciled in the cost ledger with the general ledger.

Similarly, any *expenses* which can be *directly* charged against a particular contract, such as expenses of workmen travelling to the country, insurance of particular pieces of work, &c., are so treated. The respective accounts in the cost ledger are debited with these charges, and in the general ledger charges account is credited and cost ledger account debited, it being, of course, very desirable to charge direct to a particular work anything that can be so charged, so as to leave as little as possible to be charged for indirect expenses.

We now come to the last, and perhaps the most difficult, part of the subject,—the treatment of *indirect expenses*. In all businesses and works there are certain items which cannot always be charged against certain jobs, but have to be apportioned over the whole year's work. Some of these charges are rent, taxes, lighting, heating, depreciation, interest, salaries, and others, and distribution expenses, as advertising, catalogues, &c. How are these to be apportioned? The usual way is to charge indirect expenses as a rate, arrived at in different ways according to the class of work done, and the material used. The rate of the previous year's indirect charges or oncost to the wages paid may be used as the rate for the current year's apportionment; sometimes it is the rate of oncost to material used or to wages paid and materials used that is taken. Again, the number of hours of labour has been suggested as the basis for calculation of the rate of oncost. This point requires constant checking and consideration. Where a business is increasing the rate as a rule tends to decrease as the fixed portion of such charges is being spread over a larger amount, and in a backward business it will tend to rise for the opposite reason. Taking wages as the basis of oncost, the usual method of treatment is to take the wages paid on the different jobs each fortnight, and calculate the oncost on them at the rate calculated. These oncosts are then posted to the different cost accounts in the cost ledger, while the aggregate total of them is in the general ledger debited to the cost ledger account and credited to an oncost expenses account. At the end of the year all the indirect expenses in the different accounts in the general ledger should be transferred to the debit of the oncost expenses account. If, as is extremely improbable, the account balances good and well, but if not the difference will be the amount by which the indirect charges have been over- or under-estimated when settling the rate of oncost to be applied, and the rate was accordingly too high or too low. The balance on the oncost expenses account may be transferred to the profit and loss account, or may be charged or credited to several of the larger contracts, entries to that effect being made in the cost accounts in the cost ledger and in the cost ledger account, and the oncost expenses account in the general ledger.

It will thus be seen how each job has had charged against it all the items of cost expended in the doing thereof, and the advantages of being able to obtain such information should be evident to all who are in any way concerned with manufacturing accounts, whether as principals or as auditors.

The Accountants' Magazine.

VOL. X.   JUNE 1906.   NO. 96.

Edinburgh University and Accountant Students.

IN our February number we advocated the institution of Faculties of Commerce in the Scottish Universities. Since then most of our Edinburgh readers will have read in the 'Scotsman' of 23rd and 24th April Professor Nicholson's "Plea for the Expansion of the Economic Department in the University of Edinburgh." We are pleased to see that this suggested expansion includes all the subjects which we had mentioned as necessary additions to the curriculum of the University. Professor Nicholson says nothing of establishing a Faculty, but this is comparatively unimportant. The essential thing is, in the first place to provide the funds and the teaching. The Faculty will follow. He names particularly, as subjects which require immediate attention, economic history, statistics, geography, and mercantile law. Some provision has already been made for economic history in the shape of a short summer course, and we understand that a Chair in geography is likely shortly to be established. But with regard to mercantile law, no steps have yet been taken, and it is in this and in Professor Nicholson's further suggestion that lectureships should be established in special subjects—*e.g.*, banking, insurance, and accountancy—that the accountant profession in Edinburgh is specially interested. We may observe *en passant* that we would not be satisfied with this as an ultimate solution of the problem. Accountancy as now understood is to be classed in order of importance and scope rather with finance than with banking and insurance, which are departments of finance, and we claim that it is entitled to the dignity of a fully equipped Chair. Mr Robert Fitzroy Bell recently made, in the columns of the 'Scotsman,' a similar claim for French and German, which have only lectureships at present, and in the race for professorial honours we must not be behind the other "sturdy beggars," to borrow a phrase from Mr Asquith. However, even a lectureship would be heartily welcomed in the meantime, and it remains to be considered how Professor Nicholson's proposals, if realised, could be taken advantage of in the training of accountants. In the first place, there can be no doubt that the present connection of the Edinburgh Society with the University is far from satisfactory. Students are compelled to take two classes—Scots Law and Conveyancing. Now these classes are, of course, primarily intended for law students, and are eminently suited for their purposes; but to the accountant student they are sorely disappointing. In Scots Law a very great part of the session is devoted to subjects with which an accountant, as such, has no concern; while some of those subjects which he really requires, such as bankruptcy and company law, are of necessity treated less fully than he would desire. In Conveyancing, again, he is at a decided disadvantage as compared with the budding lawyer. The latter hears of documents and phrases with which he is more or less in daily contact, but which to the accountant student are empty abstractions, and, consequently, if he does attempt to do well, he has the mortification of seeing himself come out far behind rivals to whom he is perhaps not a whit inferior intellectually. The inevitable result is that both classes are attended by most C.A. students more as a matter of form than anything else, and with the object only of securing the required number of attendances. It is even to be feared that those of artistic temperament have been known to spend their time like Darsie Latimer—" and with what excellent advantage, my note-book, filled with caricatures of the professor and my fellow-students, is it not yet extant to testify?" The present writer recollects that in his year one student read through the greater part of 'Paradise Lost' in the Law class-room—no doubt much to his improvement in literature, but not in law. The Political Economy class might be more successful, but as it is optional, and as students have generally had enough of the University when they have taken out the two compulsory classes, it is very little taken advantage of. The really serious work of preparation for the examinations—and there is no lack of such work—is done privately and with coaches or at the classes provided by the Society.

If Professor Nicholson's proposals were carried out, we think that a much more satisfactory arrangement might be made. It is not, of course, suggested for a moment that the University should provide classes expressly to relieve the Society of Accountants from the duty of educating its would-be members. Any lectureships established would have to appeal to the business and commercial community in general. A lectureship in mercantile law, however, would naturally include most of the legal subjects which the accountant requires. Accountancy, again, would cover a considerable part of the teaching required for the practical papers in the final C.A. examination, while very particular attention should be devoted to such subjects as cost accounts, which are of vital interest to commercial men. This lectureship would naturally be held by a professional accountant, and the Edinburgh Society might well, as Professor Nicholson suggests, afford it some encouragement. A lectureship on economics, but confined to the more practical parts of the subject, might also be established, not to compete in any way with the present classes, but to meet the needs of business men and others interested in the subject. Attendance at these three classes—Mercantile Law, Accountancy, and the subsidiary class on Economics—might be made obligatory on all C.A. apprentices, who would, of course, be relieved from attending the present Law classes. They might also be recommended, especially if they contemplated remaining in

Edinburgh, to attend the banking and insurance lectures, which would no doubt receive the support of the Institute of Bankers, the Faculty of Actuaries, and the Edinburgh Insurance Society. Finally, all these lectures, if they were to be of use to business men, would require to be in the evening following the example of Birmingham, or, if this was thought at first to be too violent a departure from University traditions, they might be held before business hours.

Now we shall no doubt be told that all this is rank heresy; that it is not the function of the Universities to educate the business community; that learning can have no dealings with the money-changers of the market-place; and that the hands of commerce must not touch even the hem of her garment lest they soil its purity. To this view we are most emphatically opposed as both obsolete and selfish. To bring business men into contact with the Universities is the best and perhaps the only way to relieve them of the stigma of materialism and lack of culture which has long attached to them only too justly; and it is probable also the only way to disabuse not a few cultured people of their prejudice against business, and to teach them that to be practical is not necessarily to be either vulgar or unlettered.

CAPITAL AND REVENUE ACCOUNTS: THEIR ORIGIN AND NATURE; THE GENESIS OF THE DOUBLE-ACCOUNT SYSTEM.

By JAMES B. MACDONALD, C.A., Johannesburg.

THE ORIGIN OF CAPITAL AND REVENUE ACCOUNTS.

AN interesting and instructive article on "The Co-relation of Economics and Accounting," by Mr Victor V. Branford, M.A., which appeared in 'The Accountant' on 25th May 1901, contains the following passages bearing on the origin of capital and revenue accounts:—

It is a recent discovery of economic science that capital and income are not two *kinds* of wealth, as objects in space, but are two *forms* of wealth viewed from the aspect of time—capital being a *stock* or *fund* of wealth at a given moment, and income a *flow* of wealth during an interval of time. This is an idea which has been added to the conceptions of economics within the past decade. To say that this very idea has been part of the mental equipment of accountants for at least four hundred years would be misleading, for the handling of accounts is sometimes reduced to so highly conventionalised a routine as to convey the implication that the mental equipment of the accountant is that of the well-trained collie dog. But it is impossible to avoid the conclusion that this idea was present to the mind of the medieval arithmeticians who founded the system of double-entry book-keeping, for it lies at the very basis of that system. It is the principle of division which yields the two primary operations of the double-entry book-keeper. These operations are—(1) the making of an inventory of wealth at a given moment of time—*i.e.*, capital accounts; and (2) the registration of outgoing and incoming items of wealth during a given interval of time—*i.e.*, revenue accounts. How deeply involved is the idea of time in these operations is seen in a nomenclature that was in general use down to the early part of the nineteenth century, and still survives in some trades. According to this nomenclature, the making of the inventory was called the *rest*, and the registration of outgoings and incomings the *running* accounts. As a further indication of the same kind of association might be cited the old French custom of speaking of the *bilan d'entrée* and the *bilan de sortie*. In fact, it is clear that we are here dealing with one of those elemental concrete facts of occupational experience which constitute at once the initial matter and the ultimate criteria of science.

The synthesis presented in the modern balance-sheet disguises, under a complex symbolism, the primary purpose of capital accounts. But the statement of purpose made by the earliest known writer on double-entry book-keeping still holds good to-day.

In the book ('Summa de Arithmetica, Geometria, Proportioni et Proportionalita') that has made the name of the medieval Italian monk Pacioli equally famous in algebra and in book-keeping, the merchant who might wish to keep his accounts on the double-entry system is instructed to "make a careful inventory in such a way that he writes on a sheet, or in a special book, all that in the world he possesses, movable and immovable, even if there were a thousand things: everything must be mentioned—name, designation, mark—as much as possible; for a merchant, nothing can be too clear." The merchant's initial capital account thus compiled is composed of a series of items partly qualitatively descriptive, but in every case quantitatively determined and made commensurable by assessment in money values. In so far as the capital account deals with quantitative data—and it is clear that this is its essential character—it can be called a statistical compilation in the strictest use of that word. Thus far, therefore, the work of the accountant falls within the province of statistics. In similarly generalised scientific phraseology, we might say that the compilation of revenue accounts is an essentially historical process; and moreover, since revenue accounts deal with successive records of economic values, these documents ought to be claimed as his special property by the student of historical economics.

. . . .

If we examine almost any medieval farm account, we find items enumerated which have no money value attached to them. The typical medieval farm account consists of (1) a statement of money, income, and expenses during an interval of time—*i.e.*, a revenue account; and (2) an inventory of stock, fodder, corn, &c.—in which no money values whatever are assigned either to the items or the total,—and this we are bound to consider as the capital account in a very real and literal sense. In the relatively self-contained medieval village, with its rarity of exchange and its paucity of money, accounts were partly of the nature of inventories of goods not for sale but for use only.

In fact, I think we shall not be wrong if we generalise all these cases into the following two statements: (1) Where goods are destined for consumption by their owner without the possibility of exchange, then their assessment in money value does not in any case directly measure, and only accidentally measures indirectly, their utility to the user, and consequently the only valid and legitimate "account" of them as wealth, from his point of view, must be a quantitative statement in physical terms; (2) where goods are destined by their owner for immediate use by further elaboration for ultimate sale, then records of value are of supreme importance, but records of physical quantities may be of fundamental importance.

WHAT IS A BALANCE-ACCOUNT OR BALANCE-SHEET?

In view of the explanation just given as to the origin of capital accounts, it is a fair deduction that the assets side of a balance-account is simply "a careful inventory . . . of all that in the world" the proprietor possesses. The liabilities side of a balance-account, on the other hand, is an accounting device to note the primary interest which the creditors have in such assets when reduced to a liquid form, and the residuary interest which the proprietor has in the balance. Stating this in report form, we have—

Total assets	£000	0 0
Less liabilities to the public . .	000	0 0
Balance—Proprietors' capital .	£000	0 0

In other words, a balance-account is another term for the *capital account of the business,* and is not to be confused with the lesser *capital account of the proprietor.* The capital of the business comprises not only the capital and profits of the proprietor, but also all credit or loans obtained from outside sources. A balance-sheet gives the same information in statement form as distinguished from an account proper. One occasionally meets with a non-trading association's balance-sheet described as a capital account. If the latter is used as meaning the *capital statement* of the association as a whole, it would not be incorrect to describe it in these terms, but to apply the name "account" is inappropriate, because only a ledger account, or a copy or extract from the latter, can properly be so called.

WHAT IS A REVENUE ACCOUNT?

A revenue account is a progressive record over a period of time of incoming and outgoing items of wealth, on each of which there accrues a gain or a loss.

A mere change of assets into others of equivalent value has no place in a revenue account.

Revenue account, profit and loss account, and income and expenditure account are synonymous terms, of which the first-named has the more general application, while profit and loss account is a localised term used by trading concerns, and income and expenditure account by non-trading associations.

When an accounting takes place periodically with the proprietors of a trading business, it is found most convenient to divide the revenue account into two sections:—

(a) *The profit and loss account*, showing the actual profit or loss for the year, or other period under review, and how it has accrued.

(b) *The appropriation account*, showing not only the balance brought down from the profit and loss account, but also the profit or loss accumulated from previous periods. This account also records how any profits have been disposed of or appropriated according to the wishes of the proprietors. A loss may be met by bringing back to the credit of this account any realised profits previously reserved.

The theoretical profit and loss account may be subdivided into—

(1) Trading account,
(2) Residual profit and loss account,

or into—

(1) Manufacturing account,
(2) Trading account,
(3) Residual profit and loss account,

according as the business is concerned with trading only, or with both manufacturing and trading. The manufacturing account shows the cost of production, the trading account the gross profit on trading, and the residual profit and loss account the net profit or loss on the business as a whole.

The theoretical income and expenditure account of a non-trading association may also be subdivided into
> (1) Income and expenditure account for the year, or other period under review.
> (2) The appropriation account.

Practical experience has suggested these subdivisions as a ready means of comparing and testing results. Their value, however, is much impaired if the same principles of accounting and classification be not adhered to throughout.

Genesis of the Double-Account System.

In the latter portion of the extracts, quoted above, from Mr Branford's valuable paper, one may discern the genesis of the conception of that process of accounting known as the "double-account system."

Certain property is held by the proprietor for its utility value to him, and not for the purpose of sale or exchange to other persons. It is his "fixed capital," as distinguished from the "circulating capital" which he deals in as opportunity offers. If he paid nothing originally for his "fixed capital," say land in a new country, his accounting requirements are met by recording the area and situation of his property for the purpose of identification and making known his ownership to his heirs and successors in the event of his demise. Some years later a new-comer comes along, who fancies the tilled land and situation of the pioneer's homestead, with its possibilities for producing a good income and comfortable living. He makes a bid for the farm, and his offer is accepted. The first owner has changed his intention of holding his land for the purpose of deriving an income from its use or produce. He decides now to become a dealer in landed property for the occasion. This change of intention signifies the merging of what formerly was "fixed capital" into what presently is "circulating capital." The price obtained for the property when sold is pure gain on trading, and the amount would be carried to the credit of revenue account—there being no original cost price to offset against it. The purchaser in his turn has to bethink him of some method of accounting to record his side of the deal.

Unlike his predecessor, he has paid a sum certain in money for the property, although in both cases it was acquired originally as fixed capital. The purchaser, then, has to record in his accounts not only the area and situation of his farm, but also its cost price, in order to explain the expenditure of an equivalent amount of his liquid funds, and the change of assets which has taken place. Having done so, it is immaterial to him, from an accounting standpoint, whether his farm appreciates or depreciates in market value, because he is not dealing in farms, and until he changes his intention he cannot realise a profit or a loss on the property in question.

This principle of accounting is accepted by the law in Great Britain in the case of Joint Stock Companies, because their intentions, or rather the objects for which these companies are formed, are solemnly declared and known to all persons interested before they begin to do business, and also because legal safeguards are provided against any sudden or improper change of intention. It is not so, however, in the case of private individuals or partnerships. There is no obstacle in law to their changing their intention of converting circulating capital into fixed capital, or *vice versa*, as often as they like. Consequently, the distinction in these cases is not recognised in law, but it none the less exists in fact. In practice, accountants invariably do write off estimated depreciation on the fixed capital assets of private concerns, notwithstanding that the loss is unrealised. This is due to prudential reasons, and not in pursuance of any accounting principle. The best method, in our opinion, to give effect to this, is to raise separate reserve accounts, instead of diminishing the cost price of the assets in the books as is frequently done. The reason why the entries are made is then manifest, and the criticism of acute observers like Mr Branford, who asserts that accountants follow *conventions* rather than *principles*, would, in this instance, lose its point.

THE TWENTY-FIRST ANNUAL MEETING OF THE AMERICAN ASSOCIATION OF PUBLIC ACCOUNTANTS: IMPRESSIONS OF A VISITOR.

THE American Association of Public Accountants was formed in New York in 1887. Though originally intended as an association for the whole of the United States, its operations were practically confined to New York, and up to 1896 it had only about 100 members. In that year the Legislature of the State of New York passed an Act providing for the establishment of certified public accountants. In the course of a few years several other States had followed this example, and State Societies of those who had obtained the degree had been created. An association called the Federation of Societies of Public Accountants in the United States of America was formed in 1902. Thus there were two associations ostensibly occupying the same ground; but efforts put forth for an amalgamation of the two were ultimately successful, and in 1905 a fusion of the two associations took place under a constitution mutually adjusted, and under the name of the older association.

The American Association is now the central association for the whole of the United States, and it is composed of the members of the various State Societies affiliated with it, and of certain other gentlemen, not members of any affiliated State Society, who are known as members at large.

Sixteen of the States — viz., California, Colorado, Connecticut, Florida, Georgia, Illinois, Louisiana, Maryland, Michigan, New Jersey, New York, Ohio, Pennsylvania, Rhode Island, Utah, and Washington—have now passed laws establishing certified public accountants, and the total number of C.P.A.'s in these States is about 650. Four other States — viz., Massachusetts, Minnesota, Missouri, and Tennessee—though they have no C.P.A. laws as yet, have associations of accountants affiliated with the American Association, and their total membership is about 110.

Including fellows and associates at large and honorary members, the total membership of the American Association is 734. The C.P.A.'s of the States of Connecticut, Florida, and Utah are apparently not yet connected with the Association.

As the internal laws of each State vary considerably in matters with which accountants are concerned, it is only questions of general interest to the profession that can be dealt with by the American Association. Its objects may be stated to be, by union and organisation to elevate the profession, advance its interests, bring the different States into communication one with another, and encourage the formation of societies and the passing of C.P.A. laws in every State of the union.

The affairs of the Association are administered by a board of trustees, aided by many different committees. At the annual meetings each society is represented by a delegate or delegates, whose vote is reckoned in proportion to the membership of his society. As might be anticipated, it has been found difficult to properly consider and dispose of business matters at a meeting so constituted, and important questions are as a rule "side-tracked," as they say, by being referred to a committee.

The circumstances connected with the annual meeting are not the most favourable for the satisfactory disposal of business. Most of the delegates are on holiday,—some having come great distances, perhaps from 3000 to 4000 miles,—and in many cases they are accompanied by their families. They want to meet with friends old and new, and generally have a good time. Though the proceedings last for three days, much of this time is occupied by entertainments.

Atlantic City, where the meeting was held this year, is well suited for that sort of thing. It is an enormous pleasure resort on the Atlantic coast, about two hours from New York, and one hour from Philadelphia. It is built on a sand-bank, without any natural attractions whatever except the ocean and its fresh breezes. Some thirty years ago the whole site was, I believe, not worth fifty dollars. It is now covered with enormous hotels, piers, casinos, shops, and private residences, and boasts of seven miles of continuous shore promenade known as the "Board Walk." Its resident population is about 30,000, and there are over eighty hotels and boarding-houses.

America is a country given to conventions, and Atlantic City seems to be a favourite place for them. The week before we arrived there had been one composed of some section of railway-men, attended by 6000. I noticed another composed of 1000 laundry-men. When we went to play golf near Atlantic City the caddies said they guessed we were "convention men."

Each member wears a little badge designating the body he is connected with. Before the proceedings were over we received as honorary decorations three different badges. Each of the principal societies has also a banner with an appropriate device, which is displayed on all suitable occasions.

The meetings of accountants were attended by about 240, including some thirty guests. Of this number at least fifty were ladies, who were invited to attend all the meetings, and usually did so. Among the guests were the President and two members of the English Institute, the President and Vice-President of the Incorporated Society, representatives of five Canadian societies, and five representatives of the Scottish societies.

Proceedings commenced on Tuesday, 20th October, by the presentation of credentials, reports of the trustees, committees, &c., the sitting occupying about one-and-a-half hours. This was followed by a luncheon given by the Pennsylvania Institute of C.P.A.'s, when between 200 and 300 must have been present. The room was decorated with the British, Scottish, and Canadian flags, in honour of the guests, and Scotland was specially distinguished by there being present a piper in full Highland costume in addition to the usual musicians. Between the courses national airs were played and received with tremendous enthusiasm. There were no speeches and no wines.

In the afternoon a paper on "Railroad Accounting in relation to the twentieth section of the Act to Regulate Commerce," prepared by Professor H. C. Adams, a member of the Inter-state Commerce Commission, was discussed. The paper having previously been printed and circulated, it was not necessary to read it. The same excellent plan was followed with all the papers.

With the view of remedying certain railway abuses, Congress conferred upon the above Commission power to prescribe a uniform system of accounts for the returns required by the Act, as well as power to examine the books kept by the railway companies. The paper by Professor Adams, the Statistician of the Commission, discussed from a scientific standpoint, and somewhat minutely, the manner in which certain items should be dealt with in the accounts, particularly depreciation, and the remarks which followed were largely taken up with that point. To those interested in railway accounts the paper, which appears in the 'Journal of Accountancy,' along with the other papers read, will well repay careful study.

During the afternoon the ladies took part in a "push-chair" parade on the Board Walk.

In the evening a reception and dance was given by the New York State Society of C.P.A.'s, and kept up with spirit till a late hour.

Next morning was taken up with the election of office-bearers, and in the afternoon a paper by Mr A. Lowes Dickinson, of Price, Waterhouse, & Co.'s firm in New York, entitled "Accounting Practice and Procedure," was submitted. It bore to be addressed more to the public than to practising accountants, and it discussed fully the more important functions of an accountant, pointing out how the profession might be developed in the United States. The paper showed a great deal of sound judgment and foresight, and is of special interest to British accountants.

The society of C.P.A.'s of the State of New Jersey gave a reception and tea in the course of this afternoon, and in the evening a special session was held to welcome the guests of the Association and hear short addresses from them. The messages from the Scottish societies were received with much appreciation. It was particularly interesting to the British representatives to see and hear a number of delegates from Canada, and a matter of great regret to us that we were unable to accept an invitation to meet them in Toronto.

On Thursday morning the newly elected officers of the Association were inducted, and a paper was submitted by Mr W. M. Lybrand, Philadelphia, on "The Accounting of Industrial Enterprises." This paper dealt principally with the accounts of those trading organisations to which we have applied the general term "combine," and with the special questions which arise in bringing properly together the balance-sheets of the various units composing such a concern. The various points were treated clearly and sensibly, and the paper evoked an interesting discussion.

The afternoon of Thursday was left free, and the proceedings culminated in the evening in the annual banquet or dinner of the Association, which was attended by over 200 ladies and gentlemen. The room was a large one, permitting the company to be seated at separate small tables. On this occasion our friends relaxed their usual practice of abstinence from intoxicating liquors at meals, but although there were speeches there were no toasts, as we understand them. The Chairman was, however, called the toast-master, and he introduced each speaker in a few words and said the company would now be glad "to hear from him." Apparently the subject of his observations was entirely in the speaker's discretion. One gentleman, a leading banker of New York, made his speech, which, like some others, was closely read from manuscript, a vigorous denunciation of the C.P.A. examinations. Others spoke on such subjects as "brotherly love," "reciprocity among accountant societies," &c. One guest from each of the countries represented was given an opportunity of testifying to his and his colleagues' appreciation of the Association's hospitality and kindness. The function was a brilliant one, and seemed to be enjoyed by all; although one would have supposed the ladies at any rate must have been wearied with three hours of speechifying more or less professional in character.

There is a golf club connected with the Association, and on Friday we were invited to take part in the annual tournament, at which we were also hospitably entertained. The cup for the lowest actual score was brought to Scotland.

The proceedings, apart from some pleasant private parties, were thus brought to a close, and it may be interesting in conclusion to make a few remarks on the position of the profession in the United States as we saw it. It is plain that there has been an enormous advance in recent years, especially since the passage of the C.P.A. laws, and it is probable that in the more populous commercial States the profession will now progress by leaps and bounds. There are indications that it will be largely employed by Government departments, municipalities, bankers, and others, and when an idea once takes hold in the United States it spreads very rapidly.

On the other hand, it must be owned that the professional accountant still occupies a comparatively unimportant place in America. The fact that there are only some 700 qualified men in a population of over 70,000,000 is proof of the fact. He is as yet but little known to the general public, and his uses little understood. He has also many difficulties to encounter: the difficulty of getting properly trained assistants in a country where the idea of apprenticeship or service under articles is repugnant; the difficulty of maintaining the examinations in which a high standard of pass is required; unfair competition from audit companies in which solicitors and others having work to give out are shareholders, and from crowds of untrained men who offer to work cheaply. The absence of any general control over C.P.A. legislation and qualifying examinations in the different States is also a great drawback, as the degree may represent a very different standard of value in neighbouring States.

One English visitor, comparing British with American accountants, spoke of the latter as being "in the palace of the kings," doubtless alluding to their C.P.A. laws, but the description was repudiated by the Americans themselves, and is indeed absurd. These laws, though in a different form, really gave them no more than we have enjoyed in this country for many years, and they have some disadvantages which we have avoided.

The profession is, however, progressing satisfactorily in most parts of the United States, and the American Association is doing a very great deal to help it forward; but there is no royal road to public esteem, and some years must elapse ere it can occupy in America as good a position as it does in this country.

It would be ungracious to close without referring in grateful terms to the extraordinary kindness and attention shown by the Americans to us and to the other guests. We were met on the quay at New York by the President, Secretary, and several other leading members of the Association, assisted with our baggage, and directed to our hotels. At the convention we found everything arranged for us and our rooms secured. We were introduced to everybody, and every one seemed to vie with each other in showing us attention and hospitality.

When we left New York to return, about a dozen leading accountants assembled there to wish us good-bye, and the last word we heard as our ship left the quay was their good wishes. We made the acquaintance of many able men and genuine good fellows, and we shall all long remember with the kindliest feelings our visit to the convention and our friends of the American Association of Public Accountants.

COUNTING BY ELECTRICITY.

IN modern days mechanical devices have been introduced successfully in many departments of book-keeping and mathematics, but it has not hitherto been thought possible to apply a mechanical system to the compilation of statistics where some amount of judgment is necessary before an item can be properly classified. In connection with the numerous and complicated statements which are being made up from the Scottish Census Returns of 1911, there have been introduced for the first time in this country a number of mechanical instruments, actuated by electric current, which combine in a remarkable degree various recent inventions, and perform work which to the uninitiated observer is really astonishing. The whole of the information given in the Census Returns is classified, tabulated, counted, and summed up by machinery.

As the Census sheets themselves cannot be fed into the machine, the first proceeding which is necessary is to transcribe the information given in regard to each person enumerated on to a specially designed card, of which the following is a representation:—

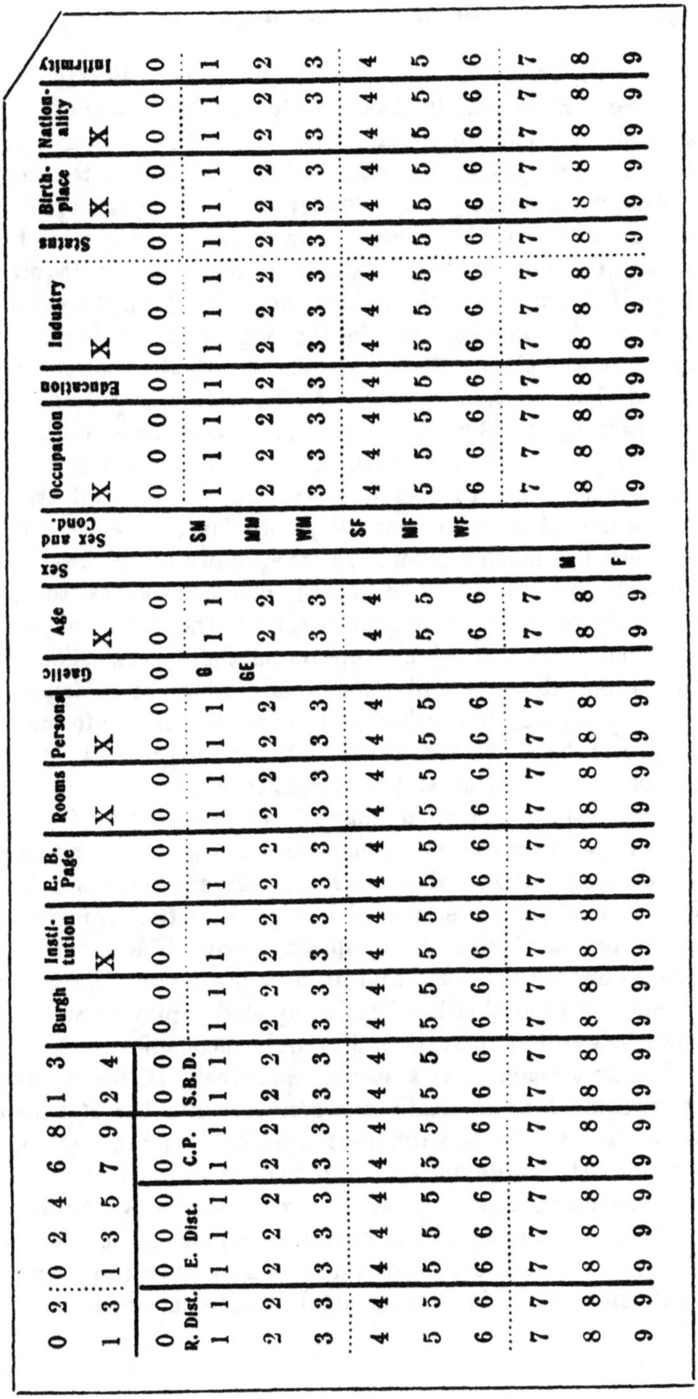

R. Dist.	0	1	2	3	4	5	6	7	8	9	1	0
E. Dist.	0	1	2	3	4	5	6	7	8	9	3	2
C.P.	0	1	2	3	4	5	6	7	8	9	5	·0
S.B.D.	0	1	2	3	4	5	6	7	8	9	7	4
	0	1	2	3	4	5	6	7	8	9	9	6
											2	8
												1
												3

Reading the card fields (rotated):

Burgh	0 1 2 3 4 5 6 7 8 9 / 0 1 2 3 4 5 6 7 8 9
Institution	X / 0 1 2 3 4 5 6 7 8 9
E.B. Page	X / 0 1 2 3 4 5 6 7 8 9
Rooms	X / 0 1 2 3 4 5 6 7 8 9
Persons	X / 0 1 2 3 4 5 6 7 8 9
Gaelic	0 G 3G
Age	X / 0 1 2 3 4 5 6 7 8 9
Sex	M F
Sex and Cond.	SM MM WM SF MF WF
Occupation	X / 0 1 2 3 4 5 6 7 8 9
Education	0 1 2 3 4 5 6 7 8 9
Industry	X / 0 1 2 3 4 5 6 7 8 9
Status	0 1 2 3 4 5 6 7 8 9
Birthplace	X / 0 1 2 3 4 5 6 7 8 9
Nationality	X / 0 1 2 3 4 5 6 7 8 9
Infirmity	0 1 2 3 4 5 6 7 8 9

65

It will be observed that everything is indicated by a number. Each county has a code number assigned to it as well as each Registration District. The various occupations, birthplaces, infirmities, &c., are designated by a distinctive number. Any number up to the space provided on the card can be recorded by punching a round hole about ⅛th of an inch in diameter over the figure required. Thus if the age, say, of the husband is 68, the figures 6 and 8 would be punched out in the appropriate column. In the exceptional case of the age exceeding 99 a special card would be required. Some of the columns provide for numbers up to 999, while in other cases only units are necessary. In order to transfer the information given on the Census sheet to a card, it is fixed into a small travelling frame above which are keys similar to the keys of a typewriting machine, and as the appropriate keys are pressed the required holes are punched so as to give correctly to any one acquainted with the code the same information as that which appears on the sheets. The card illustrated above provides for certain kinds of information being recorded, but other and more detailed information may also be tabulated, such as the numbers and ages of persons employed at stated occupations, and in such cases another card is prepared adapted for the purpose in view. It will be observed that each card has a corner removed. As different classes of cards have different corners cut off, it is at once seen when a card has got into the wrong pack, or if any card should be upside down. The cards after being punched are very carefully compared with the Census sheets, and after this has been completed it may be said that the whole of the operations are purely mechanical.

The first machine is a sorting machine. If, for instance, it is required to ascertain separately the number of persons living at each of the different ages, the machine will first sort out the cards according to the units of age, and next each group so separated according to the tens, the result being an arrangement of the cards in sequence of single ages. To effect this the cards are automatically passed one by one between a brass bar and a small magnetic brush, so that whenever the brush comes opposite the punched hole a current is set up which causes the card to be dropped into a particular slot corresponding with the number upon which the hole has been punched. In this way the cards are all arranged in separate packs, each composed of cards representing individuals of the same age. It can be immediately discovered should a card by accident have got into the wrong pack, as there should be a punched hole clear through the whole pack at exactly the same point, so that a knitting-needle can be passed through without shifting the cards. But the machine does not make mistakes, and can tabulate at the rate of about 10,000 per hour. After the cards are sorted in this way they are passed through another machine, which counts the number in each pack and also analyses the facts on one column,—for instance, if all the cards of persons aged 20 to 29 be passed through, the counter will show not only the total but also the numbers aged 20, 21, 22, 23, &c. The same system is followed in regard to all other columns in the card, and a little reflection will enable one to realise the possibilities. In fact, as soon as a card is correctly punched the machinery can be set to sort them out, so that any kind of statistical information which it is possible to prepare from the Census Returns can be rapidly and accurately made up. A machine is also employed for combining the numbers ascertained. The totals for each district are punched upon cards in the same manner as indicated above, and when these cards are passed through this machine, it automatically adds them together and shows the grand total.

It will be seen that the system, which we believe was first applied to Census Returns in the United States, is extremely ingenious and rapid in its action. It is anticipated that the work of tabulating the Scottish Census Returns for 1911 will be completed six months earlier than usual, and as the number of persons employed is naturally less, the expense may also be reduced. The use of the Tabulating Machine, the one which combines or adds the numbers recorded in the columns of the cards, is being adopted by railway companies and industrial firms for the preparation of commercial statistics.

EDINBURGH.

Society of Accountants in Edinburgh.—The Sixty-fourth Annual General Meeting of the Society of Accountants in Edinburgh was held in the Society's Hall, No. 27 Queen Street, on Wednesday, 7th February 1917. The President, Mr Richard Brown, occupied the chair.

The following Report by the President and Council was submitted:—

Early in the year, owing to the requirements of the Army, it was seen that a further depletion in the staff of the

Members of the Society was inevitable, even although the profession had been reported upon by the Scottish Committee on Substitutionary Labour as requiring special consideration. Acting upon a Memorandum received from the Secretary for Scotland in February 1916, the President and Council appointed a Committee to consider claims by Members of the Society for exemption of Assistants from military service on the grounds of their indispensability. A number of such claims were favourably reported upon to the military representative, and while temporary periods of exemption were in certain cases given, the requirements of the public service now seem to preclude any but the most urgent cases being considered. A large number of practising members of the profession have also been enrolled in the public service, and it is with much regret and sympathy that there has to be recorded the loss by death of so many Members, Assistants, and Apprentices during the past year.

Owing to the great number of Apprentices on active service, there was only one Examination during the year—viz., in June. The General Examining Board have intimated that there will be an Examination in June 1917, but that it is not their present intention to hold one in December of that year. Mr Richard Brown having resigned the office of Secretary to the Board, Mr D. Norman Sloan, C.A., Glasgow, was in February last appointed Secretary.

The Standing Committee of the Councils of the three Scottish Societies have held several Meetings during the year, and in addition to Finance and other Bills in Parliament, matters of considerable importance relating to the profession have been discussed with mutual benefit. At their last Meeting in November Mr Alexander Moore, the Chairman for the year of the Joint-Committee, presented a Silver Cup for annual competition between the three Societies in social sport, and a Committee has been appointed to arrange the nature and details of the competition. A photograph of the Cup appears in the 'Accountants' Magazine' for January 1917.

There has been a further restriction in the number of Evening Classes conducted at 27 Queen Street. Only one class for male Assistants is being held (the number enrolled being twenty-two); but, on the other hand, a course of lectures is being given to women Assistants. The Society is indebted for these lectures to Mr J. Stuart Gowans, who is kindly giving his services gratuitously. The number of students enrolled for this course is sixty-seven.

A Special General Meeting of the Society was held on the 19th July, when three new members were admitted. At this Meeting the following resolution was unanimously agreed to:—

"That the service previous to entering into an indenture in respect of which reduction in the term of Apprenticeship is permitted under Rule 32 be temporarily extended so as to include service with His Majesty's Forces during the present War, provided that any reduction in the term of Apprenticeship in respect of such service shall not exceed one year."

The business of the Society, in accordance with the arrangements made a year ago, has been carried on during the year at 27 Queen Street. After advertisement and full consideration by a Committee of applications received, Miss Jean H. Tait was appointed Assistant, to give her whole time to the work of the Society. The new arrangement has worked well, and promises to be satisfactory in every way.

There were fewer books added to the Library during the year than in the two previous years, but the new volumes include many important works, and those on the Finance Acts have been in constant demand.

In moving the adoption of the Report and Accounts the President drew attention to the fact that for the first time in the history of the Society the total membership showed a decrease. There were 584 members on the roll, as compared with 588 last year. The falling off arose from two causes, both of which are attributable to the War. The first is the fact that fewer new members—ten only—have been elected, and the second is the largely increased number of deaths, also owing to the War. Seven members had lost their lives on the battlefield, and five deaths of other members were recorded. In addition to these losses by death, two members had ceased to be members for other reasons. The number of new apprentices during the past year had been twenty-four, which is an increase upon the previous year, but is still a good deal below the average. As regards the accounts of the year, the President noted that the expenditure exceeded the income by £85. This was really better than could have been expected. It was to be feared that during the current year, in view of the very small number of new members, and of the fact that the Society is really dependent on entrance fees, the position may be worse. Matters would right themselves when the men come back, take their examinations, and join the Society. The investments had hitherto stood in the accounts at cost price. As it was thought that there was little probability of the investments recovering to cost prices, the heroic step had been taken of writing off the depreciation, amounting to £2676. A substantial reserve of £5400 was still left.

The President then referred to the difficulty experienced in carrying on business owing to depletion of staffs by enlistment. In the official documents issued it was recommended that accountants should receive the special consideration of the Tribunals. It was doubtful, as far as Edinburgh is concerned, whether enough consideration has been given. The best must be made of the situation, and all must do what they can in the circumstances.

During the year there had been several Meetings of the Joint-Committee, under the able Chairmanship of Mr Moore, the President of the Glasgow Institute. The question of the further assimilation of the rules of the three Societies had been considered. There were still some differences, and these were receiving careful attention. Another question which was being discussed by the Committee was the position of women in regard to the Society. No decision had been come to on that matter in the meantime.

In referring to the presentation by Mr Moore, the President of the Glasgow Institute, of a silver cup to the three Societies, the President expressed the cordial thanks of all to Mr Moore, and hoped that, when times are happier, the cup will be the prize in many pleasant competitions.

The President then referred to the Memorial which has been sent to the Chancellor of the Exchequer, signed by all the professional bodies in Scotland (nineteen in all), including this Society. About eighteen months ago a similar Memorial was sent, and as a result certain reforms were given effect to. That Memorial was successful in obtaining the consent of the Bank of England to dispense with the resealing of confirmations in England. The Bank of England also consented to recognise the title of a judicial factor. There were, however, other matters which it was thought should be brought to the notice of the Chancellor of the Exchequer. One was that the Bank of England refuse to recognise the official extract of a Power of Attorney. The Bank insist on getting the original and keeping it. Another was their practice of insisting on documents being executed under seal. Many bodies do not have a seal. Another point was that they will not allow the father of a child in pupilarity to deal with funds in the child's name. Then they insist upon having a certificate of the burial of a deceased person as well as of the death. Another matter was that of the fees chargeable for the certification of stock. On this the Bank of England had already given considerable concessions. Then there were the special difficulties affecting trustees in Scotland desirous of taking up Government Stock. In regard to these matters they were greatly indebted to Mr G. W. Currie, who was keeping the matter before the Government.

Another matter of interest was that the University Court have decided to institute a Degree of Commerce. There was to be either a lectureship or a Chair in the subject of Accounting. Some years ago a correspondence took place in regard to the advantages of such a class, and the President expressed the hope that the wishes then expressed may be coming a little nearer realisation.

The following office-bearers were then elected: *President*—Mr Richard Brown; *Secretary and Treasurer*—Mr T. P. Laird; *Honorary Librarian*—Mr George A. Robertson;

Members of Council — Messrs James Paterson, W. A. A. Balfour, George A. Robertson, T. Bennet Clark, J. Stuart Gowans, William Annan, Wm. Home Cook, H. D. Davidson, T. B. Whitson, D. H. Huie, Alex. Nisbet, and Eric M. Beilby; *Representatives on the General Examining Board*— The President, *ex officio;* Messrs F. W. Carter, D. N. Cotton, T. P. Laird, H. Kenward Shiells, and A. W. Robertson-Durham; *Law Agent* — Mr John L. Mounsey, W.S.; *Auditor*—Mr Edward Boyd, C.A.

Mr R. C. Millar was re-elected a Trustee on the David Murray Almonry Fund.

It was resolved to continue the grant of £40 to Edinburgh University in aid of the Class of Mercantile Law for another year.

Mr Charles William Anderson Bell, being qualified in terms of the rules and having passed the prescribed examinations, was duly elected a member of the Society.

THE APPRENTICE IN THE ARMY.

By AN APPRENTICE.

No doubt there are many men who before the war had completed two to three years of their apprenticeship, passed their intermediate examination, and who are now, after some four years of army life, beginning to turn their eyes towards things professional.

In an article I read recently concerning the return of the apprentice, it was suggested that many apprentices will be lost to the profession by reason of their staying in the army or by their seeking other employment, preferably of an outdoor nature.

From discussion with numerous apprentices at present in the army, I am able to state definitely that very few men who had commenced an apprenticeship before the war desire to break it now. Practically all are eager to return to the old life, though most have "wind-up" about their final examination, caused mainly by the feeling that they will find it difficult to settle down to serious study after the war. Most men on service find it almost a trial to read anything deeper than a modern popular novel, and practically all admit to a great lack of power of concentrating upon any subject whatsoever.

The few years spent by an apprentice under indenture previous to the war have in most cases been of great advantage to him when with the Colours. In the ranks as an N.C.O. the budding C.A. is ever in demand for detecting errors in parade states, running a battalion canteen, &c. &c. Later on, being appointed to a commission, as soon as his commanding officer hears of his pre-war employment, the one time C.A. apprentice becomes immediately an assistant mess president or the officer in charge of the Battalion War Savings Association, &c. Later again, if promotion comes his way, and he is made a company commander, he is saved much worry by the ease with which he is able to grasp army accounts and the company pay- and mess-books. Again, as an adjutant, his office training he finds invaluable in assisting him to organise an office and an office staff.

Several new departures have apparently taken place in most offices, which the apprentice in the army hears about in a vague sort of way when calling back at his old place of employment during short and infrequent periods of leave. I refer to things an apprentice hears about only by remarks made by those carrying-on at home, such as "I must get on with the Income Tax work for Messrs Profitt, Mutch & Co." The apprentice also hears in a vague sort of way that the Income Tax work done for Messrs Profitt, Mutch & Co. is a very remunerative departure for the firm. Beyond that he knows little or nothing, and that lack of knowledge makes him a trifle afraid at the thought of returning. This lack of knowledge, however, is in many instances an incentive to learn more, and that practically every apprentice realises how much it will mean to him to qualify, and qualify as soon as he possibly can after his discharge.

The large majority of apprentices in the army do *not* intend to spend much time in holidays or having a "bust" when demobilisation sets in, but taken as a whole they mean to go "all-out" for the "Final."   H. R.

THE APPRENTICE RETURNED.

By an APPRENTICE.

Not many months have elapsed since there was published in the Magazine a short article concerning "The Apprentice in the Army." During these months, however, the large majority of apprentices, who were serving, have been demobilised, and their impressions on returning to their pre-war occupations might perhaps be worthy of record.

Time, and it is rumoured the quality of the papers returned in the June examinations, have proved two things—viz., that few apprentices have elected to remain in the army, and that the large majority have quickly settled down in a manner which was as surprising to their employers as to themselves.

In the same way as benefits derived from pre-war apprenticeship training was of use in the army, so now army training is found to be exceedingly useful in the office.

Exception might be made to this by the fact that most apprentices, who have returned to their offices, display a tendency to "run the show," especially those who attained to any rank which gave them authority over others; but on the other hand, this state of affairs is much preferable to having apprentices who are apathetic and uninterested in their work.

Army discipline has also left its mark, and as the majority of returned apprentices "Sir" and pay due respect to their seniors, they also in return demand the same respect being paid to them by their juniors.

There is also a great gain in self-confidence, usually brought about by having had to stand in front of a parade and by mingling in the barrack-room or mess on equal terms with men of both a higher and a lower social standing.

There are many things that the service apprentice misses, for example, there is no guard-room in which to confine the wretched junior who has failed to finish his ledger additions within a fixed time, nor is there any kindly sergeant-major to see that the confinement is promptly and correctly carried out. Another thing much missed is the recognised ten minutes every hour "fall out for a smoke" to which he had become accustomed, but with the advent of numerous lady assistants in most offices, perhaps this "smoke business" will become replaced by afternoon tea. I think, however, that most apprentices trust it shall not be so, the prospect of living to see the day when the places of business of the Chartered Accountants of the future shall have descended into veritable teashops (where light-footed damsels trip around, and, in the intervals of taking tea and talking dress, do sundry additions and see that certain figures are the same as other figures and then go home and talk about finance) is to most service apprentices rather trying.

Regarding the attitude of employers to returned apprentices, there are few apprentices who do not say that they have received very considerate treatment, and that they are given every opportunity to undertake good work in their offices, and it lies with themselves whether they take advantage of these opportunities or not.

Again, those of the apprentices who attained, during their service, to a position of authority in the army, and there are not a few, though they at present perhaps do miss their one-time scope, cannot but admit that they, having once tasted of power, find it but an incentive to the attainment of high standing and authority in the profession of their choice.

H. R.

THE ACCOUNTANTS RELATIONSHIP WITH THE INLAND REVENUE.[1]

BY CYRIL H. TEMPLE, F.S.A.A.

I DOUBT whether in any other way the profession has progressed or gained so much in prestige as by reason of its ability to act as the *via media* between the tax-gatherer and the taxpayer. The enormous expansion and increase of taxation has brought to the profession much land for cultivation, which has yielded in manner out of all proportion to the loss of work which it was at one time thought might have ensued by the appointment of a Public Trustee.

With but few exceptions—and these must ever be present to prove the rule—the response of accountants has added much prestige to the youngest of the professions. Quite apart from the commercial aspect, invaluable help has readily been given to the country, and the benefit to the population generally has been incalculable. It is unthink-

[1] Reprinted, by kind permission of the author and publishers, from 'Pupil to Practitioner.' By Cyril H. Temple, F.S.A.A. (E. Marlborough & Co., Ltd., London. Price 3s. 6d.)

able to contemplate what would have happened during the period from 1915 to 1921 if the Inland Revenue had not possessed the advantage of a professional adviser being in so many cases retained for the taxpayer. Thereby hundreds of thousands of assessments covering Income Tax, Excess Profits Duty, Super Tax, and latterly, Corporation Profits Tax, have been speedily computed and settled, and every one left more or less satisfied. Inspectors of Taxes have on many occasions expressed to me their opinion that the accountancy profession has facilitated out of all knowledge the settlement of assessments, and thereby the collection of the various moneys without which the country could not exist.

The equation of correct assessment throws an enormous responsibility both on the shoulders of the Inland Revenue and on the taxpayer, and in a greater degree upon the accountant. The Inland Revenue are able to look after themselves, and the taxpayer may transfer most of his worry to his adviser; but the position of the accountant is a peculiar one. He is trusted by those in authority, and he must never on any account whatever, directly or indirectly, betray the confidence. It is necessary, of course, for him to be as sure as possible that the figures submitted are correct, and that he has not been misled by his client —either wilfully or otherwise. But in many instances facts come to his knowledge, and this is just where the difficulty commences; and the art of discrimination as to what should be passed on for the information of H.M. Inspector of Taxes and what should not is difficult of accomplishment.

But when once one is assured that one's duty has been performed and a clean certificate appended, on no account must one allow such figures to be challenged. If some Inspector of Taxes sees fit to do so, do not lose one moment in reporting the case to Somerset House, either to the Chief Inspector of Taxes or to the Secretary of the Board of Inland Revenue. The offence will not be repeated.

It is the fashion to-day for accounts to be subjected to many requisitions, some of which are surely unfair, unreasonable, and iniquitous. My counsel is to ignore such questions, and if they are persisted in, to report. Certain observations are necessary for a correct assessment to be computed, and the Inland Revenue should be assured of all reasonable co-operation from the accountant. I will give a sample of the kind of requests I consider unfair, all of which have actually occurred more or less recently :—

(1) Has your client, or has he ever had, a safe deposit ?
(2) Please forward a list of all the customers of your client.
(3) Please forward a list of all banking accounts of your client or his wife, and an undertaking that the list is complete, such undertaking to be signed by your client and his wife.
(4) Please let me have your client's undertaking that all gross takings will in future be banked.

And so on *ad infinitum*. All these examples, to which I could add scores, occurred in cases where no suspicion existed, and in which it was obvious that honest taxpayers were concerned.

Of quite recent date there has been established at Somerset House an inquiry branch of the Inland Revenue. It is really a miniature Criminal Investigation Department, and has been set up to recover, where possible, many sums which were undoubtedly lost to the revenue by insufficient returns made for the purposes of Income Tax or Excess Profits Duty. And now let us turn to the other side of the picture. When is some effective means of redress to be granted those who in small businesses are undoubtedly over-assessed and have at the present time no way out ?

It may be said, why not lodge an appeal to the Commissioners, either General or Special ? In the first place, these are not the kind of cases to refer to the latter, so that there is only left the General Commissioners. The treatment varies enormously according to the locality, but I will give a typical instance of a case referred to this body.

A needy widow, trading as a butcher in a poor part of Jewry, pleaded with me to take up the question of her assessment. She had been assessed at £300, and was no more making that sum per annum than she was earning £30,000. It was obviously a case where no fee could be expected, but I felt exceedingly sorry for her, and interviewed on her behalf, with herself present, the Assistant

Inspector of Taxes. He treated her most courteously, and after listening to her story, most of which I was able to confirm, he turned to me with the statement that she was obviously not taxable, and that he would recommend that the assessment be cancelled.

The poor woman was exceedingly grateful; but imagine one's surprise when, some time after, I received a letter from H.M. Inspector of Taxes stating that he regretted that the General Commissioners having made an assessment of £300 for the previous year, he was unable to recommend a reduction of this figure otherwise than by application by my client to the Commissioners.

The appeal was accordingly submitted. Result:—
  (a) A wait of nearly two hours before our case was called, during which period we were confined in the coldest and draughtiest room imaginable.
  (b) The chairman, in spite of frequent protests, was chatting the whole time to a colleague.
  (c) The Inspector of Taxes, when confronted with my conversation with his chief assistant at the earlier interview, stated he knew nothing about it.
  (d) The assessment was reduced to £275, which was just about £200 more than her net earnings.

I will not dwell further on this case, except that it is one of very many with which I have come into direct contact. Such a taxpayer is too ignorant to keep any books of account—in this case there was no banking account whatever,—and certainly quite unable to afford to employ any one to look after her financial affairs.

The method of assessments such as these is a scandal, and should be revised at the earliest moment. Personally, while retaining the Special Commissioners, for whom one has the very highest admiration, I am in favour of the abolition of the General Commissioners. I would suggest that the assessments be made by the Inspector of Taxes, and that the onus of proving such assessments should lie with the Inland Revenue, not, as at present, with the taxpayer, and that all cases of appeal be heard before the Special Commissioners, not a body of men who in so many cases possess no knowledge whatever of accounts or of income-tax law, and amongst whose members is included, very probably, a trade competitor of the appellant.

One final word concerning the General Commissioners. A client for whom personally I had much regard, but whose knowledge of matters commercial was of the slenderest—it used to take me hours to explain to him his own balance-sheet,—called upon me one day and asked me if I could give him a few tips concerning income tax, as he had just been made a member of the General Commissioners for a London district! This man had no idea of the difference between a debit and a credit, and never had the faintest idea of how his own assessment was computed. As I have said before, the whole thing is positively scandalous.

For Inspectors of Taxes as a body I have a profound respect. One must meet with the exception to give force to the rule, but the great majority are splendid men, performing a thankless task with much efficiency and diplomacy, and, in my opinion, inadequate remuneration.

At the time of writing these notes an indefinable change seems to be occurring in the relationship as between Inspector and Accountant, and I think that not a little of the irritation is caused by the Inspectors leaving so much in the hands of subordinates who possess neither the breadth of view nor the broad-mindedness necessary to settle difficult points round the table. In former years one sitting with the Inspector was alone necessary to agree on an assessment; but to-day a string of questions, many of which are quite irrelevant, are forwarded by correspondence by a junior "jack-in-office," and the irritation is set up. It is a great pity, and accountants must on their part do all possible so that matters may revert to *in statu quo ante*, to the advantage of every one concerned. And to Inspectors, may I ask that a little more personal supervision be given to the correspondence originating from the juniors?

Let us all remember that reciprocity is the soul of business.

Verification of Assets.

A paper on the Verification of Assets was read by Mr Henry Morgan, F.S.A.A., at the Autumnal Conference of Incorporated Accountants, recently held in Leeds.

Mr Morgan dealt with the duties of the professional accountant in his capacity as auditor of a limited company, and particularly with regard to his responsibility in connection with the verification of the various assets set out in the balance-sheet.

He quoted the definition of the powers and duties of auditors contained in the Companies Acts, but he pointed out that it was rather to the numerous judgments of the High Court judges in the leading cases brought before them for decision, that auditors had to look for guidance in the performance of their onerous and responsible duties.

With regard to securities, he pointed out that the Courts had refrained from laying down definite rules for the guidance of auditors, and he dealt with the difficulties which faced auditors whether or not to accept certificates of bankers, brokers and other custodians of securities, instead of insisting upon actual inspection. It was, however, wise for the auditor to satisfy himself that the documents were entrusted to the care of a " respectable, trustworthy, and responsible person," and one who, in the ordinary course of his business, would be the natural custodian of such securities—e.g., a bank. In cases where securities were deposited with custodians other than banks, an auditor should require actual inspection of the securities, if practicable.

Mr Morgan also dealt at some length with the question of window-dressing, a practice which he condemned as a reprehensible one, describing it as " a manipulation of the assets, producing a temporary change in their nature in order that the balance-sheet may convey to the shareholders and the public a sounder (and therefore a false) impression as to the financial stability of the company than would be the case if the assets were shown as they normally exist." He expressed the view that where an auditor found that window-dressing was carried on on anything like an extensive scale, it was his duty to report the matter to the shareholders.

Dealing with loans, Mr Morgan expressed the opinion

that where loans were made against undoubted security little difficulty presented itself to the auditor in arriving at a conclusion as to their value, but that where loans were made with the principal object of obliging the borrower, or to officers or directors, the most careful investigation was necessary on the part of the auditor as to the reasons for the advance and the nature of the security (if any) upon which the various loans were made, although in view of the opinions expressed by various judges in their judgments, he did not see that an auditor could be expected to value such debts any more than he could be expected to value stock-in-trade, and that he was justified in relying upon the directors' estimate of the value of particular loans. In the case of loans to directors and officers, Mr Morgan expressed the opinion that they were undesirable, and that there must always be a point at which they became improper, in which latter event the duty of the auditor was clear.

In dealing with stocks, Mr Morgan referred to the general practice amongst auditors to accept certificates of the managers in control of the business or of the different departments as to the value of stock; but suggested that the auditor should not accept such certificates without examination and inquiry and the application of such tests as are available to him, not merely as a safeguard against dishonesty, but mainly to ensure that errors of principle in regard to valuation had not been made. While stating the general principle that the stock should be valued at cost price or present market value, whichever is the lower, he advised that the auditor should make inquiry as to whether any part was surplus or obsolete stock, and see that adequate allowance had been made therefor.

The most interesting part of Mr Morgan's paper was devoted to the duty of an auditor in reporting the facts as he discovered them to the directors and to the shareholders. He stated that it was a common practice for the auditor to settle the balance-sheets of public companies with the secretary or chairman or managing director, with the result that the auditor never came in personal touch with the directors as a whole. He strongly advocated that after his examination of the company's books and documents, the auditor should submit a full and detailed report in writing to the board of directors for their consideration, dealing with matters arising in the course of the audit, and particularly with regard to matters upon which the auditor was in doubt or difficulty, inasmuch as the directors shared with the auditor the responsibility for the issue of a true and correct balance-sheet, and that directors should be afforded the advantage of meeting and consulting with the auditor in order to arrive at such a result.

He pointed out that the provision in the Companies Act for a report by the auditor to the shareholders was practically a dead letter, for the reason that the disclosure of confidential information to the public would have injurious effects on the company's interests. There could, however, be no objection to the issue of such a detailed report to the directors, which should deal fully with all items in the balance-sheet, and in the case of the assets set forth the methods adopted for the purposes of verification. He strongly urged that auditors should be required to attend the board meetings when the balance-sheet was to be submitted to the directors for approval, and expressed the opinion that if such a course of procedure were made obligatory there would be much less risk of any one or two directors committing such frauds as have been the subject of recent judicial inquiry, where the frauds had been rendered possible only by reason of the other directors being kept in ignorance by the fraudulent director of what was really transpiring.

Finally, Mr Morgan dealt with the report of the auditor to the shareholders, and expressed the opinion that while an auditor should not err, on the one hand, by reporting matters which were for the directors to deal with, and which might cause injury to the general body of shareholders if discussed in public, he should not shrink from the necessity of reporting serious matters to the shareholders in language so clear as to admit of no doubt in the mind of a shareholder of average intelligence.

AMERICAN UNIVERSITIES AND THE TEACHING OF COMMERCE.

By W. T. BAXTER, B.Com., C.A.

A UNIVERSITY education is now as necessary a part of the average middle-class American's equipment as his automobile or refrigerator. In consequence, there are not far from one million students in the United States, distributed over nearly a thousand institutions aspiring to university or college status. Incidentally, the names 'university' and 'college' are here used indiscriminately, as they indicate nothing except the personal taste of the namers.

It is inevitable that the quality of the teaching should vary enormously when there are so many different institutions concerned. Not more than a score of them can be regarded as having achieved levels comparable with those of most European universities. There is a tremendous gap between, say, Harvard and the Baptist college set up by some 'hick village' out in Arkansas. This dissimilarity has been accentuated not only by geographical factors, but also by the various methods in which an academic institution may be governed. Some universities are autonomous, having been privately endowed; some are controlled by the State in which they are situated; and some are under the thumb of a religious body. Usually the first type is the most scholarly, and the last the least.

Even the depression has not materially affected America's wholesale demand for college degrees, although acute suffering has been caused not only to many of the students, but also to some of the professors. Education is by no means a sheltered industry in the United States. Those universities which are dependent upon State grants have had their incomes slashed in the most merciless fashion, particularly in the numerous States which are dependent upon agriculture for their revenues. (Since 1927 about a quarter of the farms in America have been seized because their owners are hopelessly in debt, and now many of the farmers are so desperate that no tax-collector who prizes a whole skin dares to demand a cent from them.) A professor in a State-maintained university told me that he was daily expecting a *second* cut of 50 per cent in his salary. A few of the worst-hit colleges are accepting fees paid in kind, and the students bring along corn or cattle when they come to enrol.

It is perhaps characteristic of the United States that education there has always been strongly utilitarian. In the eighteenth century, when European universities were teaching only Greek, Theology and kindred subjects, the Americans were already breaking away from this classical tradition and were boldly introducing into their curricula subjects which had some bearing upon daily life. Benjamin Franklin was the pioneer in this, as in so many other matters; the college which he set up in Philadelphia taught not only conventional subjects, but also the sciences, including book-keeping. Ever since, Americans have continued to enlarge the scope of their higher education; and while we may sneer at college classes for ' morticians ' and ice-cream makers, nevertheless our own universities have benefited greatly from watching the American experiments, and often have ultimately adopted something of value from the new-fangled courses.

Remembering these twin facts—that a college training is quite normal in the United States, and that education there tends to strike a strongly utilitarian note—one is not surprised to learn that commerce degrees are held by a far larger percentage of business men in America than in Britain. I think I am safe in saying that the majority of the transatlantic universities now teach commerce, or, as it is more generally called, Business Administration. Sometimes the course extends over four years and is intended for undergraduates, and sometimes it is compressed into two years and is only available to students who already hold an Arts or other preliminary degree.

Exactly twenty-five years ago Harvard, the oldest and in many respects the most attractive of America's universities, aroused bitter feelings among its more conservative members by setting up a Business School. Even to-day one meets plenty of Harvard graduates who feel that their Alma Mater betrayed her best traditions when she undertook to teach Commerce. However, the disfavour of ' pure ' scholars has not prevented the new institution from flourishing, and now it is quite a picturesque feature of America's academic life.

The Harvard Business School is peculiar in a variety of respects. It restricts its enrolment to twelve hundred, and so is able to pick and choose its students, since far more than that number wish to attend it. Applicants for admission must already hold a bachelor's degree, and are supposed to have done some Economics. No women students are tolerated. Thanks to a vigorous drive for funds in the pre-depression era, the School is very wealthy, even according to American standards, and it has been able to spend lavishly on its buildings. These stand among sports fields, and are separated from the rest of the University by a wide river; there are about half a dozen dormitories, a large block of offices for the staff, and the main structure containing the library and classrooms.

But the most interesting feature about the school is its method of teaching. It relies exclusively on what is known as the ' Case System.' This system is based upon the study of concrete illustrations from real life instead of general principles. It was first developed in Harvard Law School, where the staff believe that students can best learn any branch of law, not by reading the broad theory and then applying it to actual cases, but by studying first the actual cases and then deducing the theory for themselves. Possibly such a system is quite suitable for teaching law, but it is doubtful whether it is the best method for giving instruction in Commerce, which, of course, lacks anything comparable with the great body of easily accessible legal decisions which may be used by the Law School as its raw material. The Business School has had to collect its own raw material. Thanks to its wealth, and to the co-operation of manufacturers and financiers, it has been able to accumulate a mass of information bearing on every type of business activity. Young graduates are sent out as 'field workers' to make studies of industrial and commercial undertakings; naturally, care is taken only to select firms whose organisation or methods are likely to illustrate some general principle of Economics which the School staff is anxious to emphasise. Usually the management of a firm will, after suitable coaxing, permit the investigation, provided that the information obtained is submitted to the students in such a fashion that the identity of the business cannot be discovered; sometimes, however, the stipulation is made that a certain period of years must elapse before the information is used.

The reports of the 'field workers' are the 'cases,' and groups of similar cases are published together. So when a Business School student buys his text-book for any class, he finds that it contains, not a discussion of general principles, but a series of independent chapters, each of which describes under an assumed name the circumstances of a real business. Before each meeting of the class the students are told to read one of the chapters and to think over certain questions regarding the conduct of the undertaking described therein. At the class these questions are discussed lengthily, until at last some sort of decision is arrived at as to the best course of procedure for the firm in question.

Let me give an example of the working of the system. The Professor of Accounting, shall we say, wishes to familiarise his students with a certain kind of cost-accounting. Instead of contenting himself with a talk on general principles, or with concocting a description of some imaginary company, he obtains full particulars as to the work of a real undertaking. These particulars are set forth with much detail in a case, which is published as part of the text-book on 'Problems in Industrial Accounting.' Before the lecture the students read this case. At the lecture the Professor says: "Now, gentlemen, you know the kind of work carried on by the Blank Quarrying Corporation. Tell me exactly what its accountant must do in order to establish a satisfactory cost system." The students make their suggestions, the Professor criticises and modifies them, until at last a complete cost ledger has been drawn up on the blackboard.

It will be seen that the case system differs considerably from the usual methods of teaching. Much controversy arose over it at its inception, and fierce arguments are still taking place as to whether it is superior to ordinary lecturing. In its favour the statement is made that students who have been trained to deal with cases are well equipped to tackle the problems with which they will be confronted in real business. Probably also the lessons are more vivid and comprehensible. For instance, the accountancy students who were present at the lecture described in the preceding paragraph were compelled to ponder for some time over the circumstances of a rather peculiar type of business, and in the end would very likely be able to visualise its accounts in a much clearer fashion than if they had merely listened to a general talk on costing methods.

On the other hand, the case system is exceedingly expensive to start. Often a great deal of reading has to be done by the students before a minor principle can be elucidated. And unless the professor periodically reviews a series of cases, and shows what general principles it is meant to illustrate, there is a grave danger that the students will never suspect the existence of the general principles. After all, the essence of scientific thinking—which is presumably what a university is trying to inculcate—is the reduction of masses of facts to something simple and general. If the case system results in minds well stored with disconnected facts, but unable to discipline these facts into orderly array, then students will emerge from the Business School less educated than when they entered it.

It is probable that many of the teachers do in practice modify the system by intermingling ordinary lectures with the cases. At any rate, despite the adverse criticism which can be levelled at the School's system of instruction, most of its graduates do not seem to encounter undue difficulty in finding posts.

One of the most interesting features of the School's research work is its investigations into the cost of running certain types of shops, such as department and chain stores. These studies are made in co-operation with trade associations, which invite their members to submit full annual accounts to the School. Needless to say, the data obtained is regarded as confidential, and is only published in manners which make it quite impossible to discover information about any specific business. Typical figures for each class of expense (*e.g.*, wages), and for the rate of stock turnover, &c., are worked out for each type of shop. The firms which submit accounts are provided with a report showing the results of the study, and in this way can compare their own efficiency with that of the rest of the trade.

The results are further analysed to show figures for stores with large and with small sales, for stores situated in big and in little cities, and so on. In this way facts are obtained concerning economic phenomena about whose nature we could otherwise only guess.

It is unfortunately characteristic of many American universities to spend much money on physical equipment and but little on salaries. As a result, the 'faculty' are often underpaid in comparison with persons doing other kinds of work, and this has naturally affected the calibre of the teaching. On the other hand, not only are the buildings attractive, and even grandiose, but they also tend to be expensively equipped. Thus the libraries are normally well stocked and possess elaborate mechanical devices, such as automatic book conveyers; 'elevators' are regarded as necessities; and the statistics classes are provided with formidable batteries of electric calculating machines.

The visitor to American universities may then, I think, legitimately criticise their emphasis on physical rather than mental furniture, and—with still greater validity—their tendency to sacrifice quality to quantity. Nevertheless he must in justice add that the same universities often display considerable originality in their methods of instruction, that they keep in the closest touch with business, and that they by no means confine their services to teaching. Moreover, no matter how much one may regret the over-democratic spirit which permits large numbers of ill-equipped persons to become students, one cannot but believe that these persons profit in some measure from their training, and that in the long-run American business will derive substantial benefit from the wholesale higher education of its future executives.

LEGAL NOTES.
SELECTED CASES.
HUSBAND AND WIFE.
Smith v. Smith.

Husband and wife—Property—Wife's savings from household funds.

A FAMILY consisting of the husband and wife and several children lived together. The husband and children made contributions to the wife for household expenses. The wife having obtained a decree of judicial separation against her husband, he brought an action against her for payment of the money she had saved from the sums contributed.

Held that, in the absence of any special arrangement on which the children made the contributions to their mother, these contributions must be assumed to have been made to her for their maintenance in their father's house, and therefore to have been received by the wife as *praeposita rebus domesticis*, and accordingly that the husband was entitled to the savings.—(Court of Session.)

DONATION.
Hubbard v. Dunlop's Trustees.

Donation—Corporeal moveables—Possession.

A mother handed her daughter a letter in these terms: " As I go out so little nowadays I should like to give you,

THE DUNLOP RUBBER COMPANY ACCOUNTS.
By W. F. EVA, C.A.

THE report and accounts of this company have just been published and make interesting and cheerful reading. The shareholder will note that his dividend is doubled at 8 per cent, while over 13 per cent was earned on his shares. This side of the accounts is reviewed in this month's Investment Notes. The accountant will congratulate the shareholder and proceed to examine the accounts with interest and admiration, for at last one of Great Britain's largest combines has dared to lift the veil and presented us with accounts which are clear and informative. It has submitted, along with the usual statutory requirements, a consolidated statement of assets and liabilities of the company itself, its subsidiaries and sub-subsidiaries, and also a consolidated statement of profits.

It is unfortunate that at this late date we should have to hail these accounts as "unique," "a new departure" and "an example to other companies," but it is a fact that these expressions are true and that there is no general tendency among the large British companies to present their accounts in such a way that the true position is disclosed. So complex have many large companies become, with subsidiaries and sub-subsidiaries and in some cases an even longer family tree, that the accounts as usually submitted to shareholders, showing only dividends, if any, from immediate subsidiaries, are completely uninformative and misleading. In this respect we in this country are far behind the Americans, who do not appear to be so reticent about the affairs of their large corporations. This is not a new subject, and it is surprising that more headway is not being made towards the clearer presentation of company accounts. One may feel sure accountants are not to blame for this lack of progress; in fact, the opposite may be stated, that accountants seem to be the only people who are really interested in this matter. The legislature as evinced by the last Company Act is not enthusiastic about it and only timidly recognised the existence of subsidiary companies, while it completely ignored the possibility of sub-subsidiaries. It did not recognise the fact that so many subsidiaries are made private companies with all the shelter they afford for not publishing plain and straightforward accounts. The main offenders appear to be the heads of the companies themselves, who apparently consider it advisable to keep the public in perpetual ignorance as to their affairs. Of course it may be argued that the preparation of consolidated accounts would be impracticable in the case of large companies, but Dunlops give the answer to that objection, for its accounts embrace some ninety companies with total assets amounting to over £29,000,000. Also it may be asked, that if a company is so large as to prevent the presentation of proper accounts to its proprietors can such a company be managed efficiently and should such a company be allowed to exist? There was published in last month's issue a lecture by Mr L. B. Bell, C.A., in which he made some critical and pertinent remarks on this very subject.

The accounts of the Dunlop Rubber Company are complete in every way. There is published, of course, the statutory balance-sheet, which is very fully described and grouped. The corresponding figures for the previous year are given at the side for comparison, and this is a most useful feature which could be given in all companies with the greatest of ease, despite their size. The profit and loss account is also fully stated with comparative figures for the previous year. Then follows the consolidated statement of assets and liabilities. A special feature of the Dunlop accounts, however, is the statement of consolidated profits. This is perhaps the most useful document submitted, yet, strangely enough, it is the one most usually omitted by companies which publish consolidated balance-sheets.

As Mr Bell points out in his lecture, the legislature has made a considerable number of regulations about the balance-sheet, but the profit and loss account was not even mentioned in the Company Acts prior to 1929, and even in the 1929 Act the profit and loss account is only mentioned by name. There are no regulations as to its form or contents. While, of course, an informative balance-sheet is essential to the correct assessment of a company's position, its earning capacity is of vital importance, as it is on this that the real value of the balance-sheet depends. This reluctance to give profit and loss details extends also to consolidated accounts. There are several large companies which publish a consolidated balance-sheet, but its value is greatly diminished by the omission of a consolidated profit and loss account. For example, the accounts of Turner & Newall Ltd. are very informative. Like Dunlops, comparative figures are given along with a consolidated balance-sheet and a schedule of the company's investments and a copy of the speech which the chairman is going to read at the ensuing general meeting. Thus the shareholder has before him in one document a nearly complete statement of the company's position—only a consolidated profit and loss account is missing. It is to be hoped that, following the example of the Dunlop Company, this will make its appearance next year.

As the publication of consolidated balance-sheets and profit and loss accounts is so rare, and as the ordinary text-books have as yet paid little attention to this subject of accounting, it might prove interesting to reproduce here in an abbreviated form the consolidated accounts of Dunlops. I have condensed those items which have no interest from a 'consolidated' point of view, but printed in full those that have.

DUNLOP RUBBER COMPANY, LTD.

CONSOLIDATED STATEMENT OF ASSETS AND LIABILITIES AS AT 31ST DECEMBER 1933—incorporating the figures of the audited Balance-Sheets (after elimination of inter-company balances) of the Dunlop Rubber Company, Ltd., and all subsidiary and sub-subsidiary companies in which the Dunlop Rubber Company, Ltd., and any of its subsidiaries hold over 50 per cent of the Ordinary Shares or Stock of those companies or over 50 per cent of the voting control.

Assets.

I.	Fixed assets		£15,564,617
II.	Investments at cost, less amounts written off—		
	(a) Investments in associated companies . . .	£977,087	
	(b) British Government securities	89,265	
	(c) Trade and sundry investments	129,285	
			1,195,637
	Carry forward . . .		£16,760,254

	Brought forward	£16,760,254
III.	Current assets	11,336,708
IV.	Goodwill Accounts, including the difference between the values at which inter-company holdings of shares are taken as assets into the Balance-Sheets and their par values *less* undistributed profits at the date of the acquisition of such shares	1,323,663
		£29,420,625

The investments in associated companies are, of course, not subsidiaries as defined above, but will constitute large holdings nevertheless in companies which may eventually become subsidiaries.

Note that included in Goodwill is the adjustment between the par value and the value as taken into the balance-sheet of inter-company holdings of shares, and also the adjustment for pre-acquisition reserves.

Liabilities.

I.	Share capital of Dunlop Rubber Company	£12,251,045
II.	Surplus and reserves	4,614,871
		£16,865,916
III.	Interest of outside shareholders—Preference and Ordinary Share Capital of subsidiaries held by outside shareholders, after taking into account their proportion of General Reserves and Undistributed Profits or Losses attributable thereto	6,153,496
IV.	Debentures, mortgages and loans	3,125,884
V.	Current liabilities	3,269,674
VI.	Suspense Account for transactions with subsidiary companies between the dates of their Balance-Sheets and 31st December 1933	1,284
VII.	Exchange Suspense Accounts	4,371
		£29,420,625

The total assets and liabilities of the parent company and all its subsidiaries and sub-subsidiaries are incorporated into the consolidated statement, and in order to adjust for the rights of the shareholders outside the controlling group their capital holdings along with their proportion of general reserves and undistributed profits, less losses, are aggregated as a liability as shown above in item III.

The consolidated Profit and Loss Account is as follows:—

STATEMENT OF PROFITS FOR THE YEAR 1933.

I. The aggregate profits of the Dunlop Rubber Co., Ltd., for the year 1933, including its proportion of the profits, *less* losses, of all subsidiary and sub-subsidiary companies, after providing for depreciation, &c., but before providing for Guaranteed Preference Dividends of subsidiary companies, amount to . £2,255,973

II. In addition, the Dunlop Company's proportion of various items which do not represent normal earnings attributable to the current year, amounts to 90,671

III. Aggregate total £2,346,644

IV. From the results of subsidiary and sub-subsidiary companies included above there has been deducted—
   (a) The Dunlop Rubber Company's proportion of British and foreign taxation paid by or provided in the accounts of such companies . . £229,440
   (b) Payments of subsidiary companies' Preference dividends . . 164,859
   (c) The Dunlop Rubber Company's proportion of special appropriations and undistributed profits of the year held in reserve 83,421
                                                477,720

V. Balance available to the Dunlop Rubber Co., Ltd. (as shown in that company's Profit and Loss Account) £1,868,924

VI. Deduct—
   (a) Guaranteed dividends required to be met by Dunlop Company . . £70,882
   (b) Interest on Company's Debentures . . . 285,176
                                                356,058

VII. Leaving net profit as per Dunlop Rubber Company's Profit and Loss Account . . £1,512,866

It is to be noted that the aggregate profits from all

sources is shown less losses, and in order to reconcile this figure with Dunlops' own Profit and Loss Account, there is deducted the proportion of tax paid by subsidiaries applicable to the Dunlop holding, the dividends paid to outside shareholders, and also the proportion of reserves and undistributed profits of the year applicable to the Dunlop holding. The latter deduction is the important feature of consolidated profit and loss accounts. This gives the clue as to whether the subsidiaries are earning their dividends or whether the parent company is taking dividends from one company which is making a profit while the group as a whole is making a loss. Without this statement all that we would know from Dunlops' own accounts would be that the net profit was £1,512,866, but the consolidated account tells us that after paying dividends to the parent company there was £83,421 of undivided profits applicable to Dunlops left in the subsidiary companies as a whole. It would appear, therefore, that in this case the subsidiary companies are paying away practically all their profits in dividends to the Dunlop Company.

Another noteworthy feature of this consolidated statement is the candid reference to certain items of non-recurring income. The cynics may say, of course, that it is pleasant and easy to be informative when things are going well, but Dunlops have steadily been building up a good reputation and having once created this precedent in publishing really informative accounts it would be a bad blow to the company's prestige should it revert to the old methods. Of course, the directors have to be wholeheartedly behind a change such as this, because it must be remembered that if the directors are determined to conceal any particular information they could no doubt find ways and means of doing it.

About the only other company which publishes really complete consolidated accounts is the well-known papermaking firm of Wiggins, Teape & Co. With the examples of Dunlops and this company before them, perhaps our legislators will do something to enable the public to get clearer and more satisfactory accounts, unless, of course, public opinion induces such companies as Shell, Imperial Tobacco and Imperial Chemical Industries voluntarily to give the information required.

THE ACCOUNTANT AND THE MACHINE.
By C. RALPH CURTIS, M.Sc.(Econ.).

THE very great strides which have taken place in the technique of office organisation during the past ten years have laid a heavy burden of responsibility on to the shoulders of the accountancy profession in several directions. At the same time a new subject has been added to the accountancy curriculum, a subject which, although it does not yet figure in the examination syllabus—and that will surely come—is none the less one of paramount importance for the young accountant, whether he be thinking of entering practice or of utilising his training in the commercial world.

With regard to the problems of machine accountancy, it must be remembered that the accountant in practice is both an auditor and an accountant. I have never yet seen the difference between the auditor and the accountant defined, but a simple definition would be to say that whilst the auditor audits the books the accountant keeps them. The distinction is more important than would at first sight appear, and the attitude of the professional accountant towards machine accounting must be coloured by the fact that he may be regarding these problems with a bias towards one side or another. *Qua* auditor, the accountant is concerned with the effects of machine accounting on his audit. In how far can he accept the machine figures as correct? What are the possibilities of human error, still more what are the possibilities of a protection against fraud? How far is the posting from one book to another completely automatic, and in consequence how much of his detailed check can be dispensed with? This and many similar questions are constantly arising when the subject is looked at from the point of view of the auditor.

From the accounting point of view, it must be remembered that the merchant or manufacturer who wishes to obtain the latest details as to the improvements which have taken place in production technique in his particular line usually goes for advice to the practising industrial engineer. When, however, he wishes to obtain information as to the latest developments in the technique of office organisation, he should have an expert in this connection ready at hand to give the necessary advice. Sometimes he gets it from his auditors and sometimes not. If these accountants are either not in a position or are not eager to advise, he frequently turns in despair to the machine salesman, and is at once lost. The salesman is intent only on selling his machine, irrespective of the fact that it may or may not be the right machine for the job. All makes of machines can be adapted for every machine-accounting job, just as a square peg can eventually be forced into a round hole if the hammer be heavy enough. This does not mean, however, that every machine is suited for every job. I will say at the outset that no one make of machine can be said to be better than any other. They all have their peculiar characteristics which make each of them more suitable for some particular job, and it is the expert's job to find the right machine and to fit it to the work to be done.

Most accountants are familiar with the disgruntled business man who has installed a machine-accounting system and has been very disappointed and very dissatisfied with the results. In nearly every case such dissatisfaction can be traced to the fact that the customer has yielded to the blandishments of some particularly silver-tongued machine salesman, with the result that the wrong machine has been employed, and although the work has been done mechanically, it has by no means been done in the easiest or most efficient manner. Many of the firms marketing these machines have recognised this fact, and have been quick to see that one dissatisfied user is a bar to progress for all firms selling office equipment. They have, therefore, by a process of assimilation or amalgamation, acquired the rights over machines of differing characteristics, so that their salesmen have a range of machines to choose from when advising as to the introduction of machine systems.

However this may be, it would seem that the accountant is the proper person to whom the business man should be able to turn for advice in this connection, and it is to be feared that the profession as a whole has not been quick to seize this opportunity as it might well have done.

Let us consider the matter first from the point of view of the auditor. The process of routine checking involves an almost soul-searing task whereby every entry into a set of prime books is checked by hand against the original documents, and then rechecked when it is transferred to the personal ledgers, with possibly a third check when the impersonal ledgers are being examined. I have not the least doubt that the older members of the profession will claim that it is this grounding in routine checking which makes and trains the careful and exact accountant in later years. It may perhaps be set down to the impetuosity and inexperience of youth if I venture to challenge the truth of such a statement.

How far, then, do the machines do away with the necessity for routine checking ? The answer to this question depends upon the system employed, and it is one which it is impossible to answer dogmatically. If the auditor can obtain from a reasonable number of the customers and suppliers of the concern written agreement as to the balances on their accounts, I would suggest that even the check from the original documents to the prime books is unnecessary. I am aware that such an idea will be regarded in some quarters as being completely revolutionary, but I am convinced that much time is taken up in checking original documents which mean nothing at all.

Take, for example, the case where the invoices and sales day book are being posted in one operation, and the copy of the invoice is used as a voucher for the posting of the sales ledger. It is presumed that the sales day book will be provided with analysis columns corresponding to the different sales ledgers. If, therefore, the debit totals on the daily proof sheets in the ledger-posting machines for each individual ledger agree with the daily total of the analysis column of the sales day book for the same ledger, then there is a proof that every invoice has been posted to a ledger account. In the same way, if the credit totals on the ledger machine proof sheets agree with the different totals of the analysis columns in the bank book, then there is a proof that every payment received has been credited to an account. These machine totals are automatically produced, and cannot be 'wangled' by the machine operator.

It is then simply necessary to check the daily proof sheet totals of the bank book with the pass book to be absolutely certain that every penny which has been paid into or drawn out of the bank has passed over a ledger account. If, therefore, after having first checked them against the ledgers, the auditor insists on himself posting the statement off to the clients, at the same time requesting them to answer direct to him and not to the concern, he can be sure that any mistake or frauds which are concerned with the customers' accounts will be discovered at once. He need not fear if all the customers do not return their agreement, for he can feel fairly sure that all those whose statement contain errors will write at once to protest, whilst those who do not write will be in agreement, but will probably not be desirous of paying at once.

The main thing is that with a properly organised machine system it is impossible to enter cash either in or out of the bank book without at the same time crediting or debiting a ledger account, and it is also impossible to enter an invoice into the sales day book without debiting a client. If there is a collusion between a clerk in the office and a customer, it is an easy matter to establish a fictitious invoice at an absurd price, but no manual check in the world by the auditor other than that of comparing the prices on each invoice will bring such a fraud to light. Such a fraud is, however, made almost impossible if invoices are typed on book-keeping machines in one operation with the sales day book. In such cases the invoices are done in quadruplicate, one as an original, one as a filing copy, one as a voucher for the ledger clerk, and the last one as a voucher to the packing department. Under such circumstances it would be almost impossible to establish fictitious prices for goods without someone noticing it, as the copies would be handled by four or five different persons.

Where the punched card system is employed for accounting purposes, still less checking is required. Once the original card has been punched, the whole of the remaining work is completely automatic. If sales cards are punched from the invoices and from the cash payments, then sales ledgers, sales day books, bank journals, all can be produced without any human interference and with no possibility of error. In addition to this, the one possibility of error in other machine systems—posting to the wrong account in the right ledger—becomes almost an impossibility, as the tabulator and sorter 'sense' the clients' account number on the punched card, and the former will only print and add together cards with the same clients' account numbers punched into them.

Any lingering doubts which the auditor may have as to the necessity for checking up the invoices against the original cards can be completely dispelled if either of two ideas are adopted, along with the punched card. In the first case the invoices are themselves prepared automatically on an alphabetic tabulator from cards which have either been punched from the order sheet or have been pre-punched in advance to form a stock control analysis, and are 'pulled' from there as the goods are sold. In such cases there is little for the auditor to do except to obtain the customer's agreement and to use the machine totals provided by the tabulator to frame the final accounts. In the second instance, double punching is used by the firm to make sure that the original card has been correctly punched. In such cases two different operators punch independently the same card from the same printing material. The second operator is, however, provided with a punch which is slightly offset in such fashion that all the circular holes which are already in the card are converted into ovals. If either of the operators disagree, there will be one or more circular holes left in the card. It is not, however, necessary to search the cards for circular holes, as a machine has been invented into which all cards thus punched can be placed and which will run through the cards at an almost incredulous speed, and will throw in automatically a red card alongside every card bearing a circular hole.

Once the auditor can be convinced that he can depend upon the machine figures in what I may call the routine part of the audit—personal ledgers, prime books, invoices, &c.—he will then be able to devote his whole attention to the loopholes which still exist for error or fraud—charges of various kinds, expenses, stock valuation, and stock amortisation—matters with which no machine system can deal, but which frequently need very careful rechecking.

Even in these matters there are many ways in which a machine system can assist the auditor, but these belong more properly to a discussion of the accountant's problems *qua* accountant rather than *qua* auditor. I hope to have the opportunity of elaborating this side of the problem—a side in which many thousands of pounds can sometimes be saved for customers—in a later issue.

PRINCIPLES UNDERLYING PROFIT STATEMENTS AND BALANCE-SHEETS.

By IAN W. MACDONALD, C.A.,
PROFESSOR OF ACCOUNTANCY AT THE UNIVERSITY OF GLASGOW.

(*Being the Inaugural Lecture as Professor of Accountancy delivered on 10th October* 1938.)

PROBABLY the accounting documents most widely studied are the profit statements and balance-sheets of commercial and industrial undertakings. It may be of general interest to attempt a short analysis of some of the principles underlying these documents.

Speaking as a practitioner, it has been my experience that while we deal with many balance-sheets and profit statements, the nature of our practical work does not compel us to think in terms of principles. To a large extent we work from rules and conventions, which we accept without question and apply to each specific case with which we deal. We frequently have problems to solve and difficulties to overcome, but we endeavour to meet these by concentrating on the factors relevant to each case. Our approach is specific—not general. We are concerned with one balance-sheet—and then another—but not with all balance-sheets. Many of us are so absorbed by our practical work that we have neither time nor opportunity for scientific reflection. I think you will agree that if a science has to develop from a practical basis—as accounting must—it is essential that some of the mental energy of practitioners and students be devoted to the building of an adequate theoretical structure. It is doubtful if this task has so far received the support which it merits.

I propose to adopt a negative method of approach by first considering some of the limitations of profit statements and balance-sheets as sources of information. This method is chosen deliberately, as it is difficult to construct a positive analysis owing to the lack of uniform treatment by accountants of the information which materially influences the final answers. As an illustration of this difficulty there is no accepted accounting terminology. Vital words such as 'profit,' 'income,' 'assets,' &c., are not used with the degree of precision or uniformity necessary for a positive analysis. For example, it is obviously not possible to say that all profit statements will show this or that when there is a varying meaning and conception of 'profit.' This is not intended to imply that 'profit' is necessarily capable of precise definition. These observations are merely given by way of comment on present-day terminology difficulties.

LIMITATIONS OF PROFIT STATEMENTS AND BALANCE-SHEETS.

Using the negative approach, let us consider some of the things that these statements do not usually show :—

1. The statements are not entirely summaries of fact. Estimates are also included. This implies the possibility of error. The greater degree of estimate involved, the wider must be the margin to be allowed for error. Therefore the statements should not be considered as accurate in a mathematical sense of the term.
2. The profit ascertained for a particular period does not necessarily relate solely to that period. The circumstances of former or subsequent periods may be reflected in the results. There is not therefore the time precision that one might expect from a reading of the conventional description of the final result—for example, "Net Profit for 1938."
3. The balance-sheet is not usually intended to show the present money value of the undertaking. The valuation attached to permanent assets such as land, buildings, and machinery, is usually related to acquisition cost, and is not necessarily any indication of the present value of these assets if the business was sold. The present worth may be greater or less. If greater, we say there is a goodwill value, which is not included in the balance-sheet.

If less, it implies that the expressed amount of the capital (*i.e.*, excess of assets over liabilities) is not intact.

4. The statements issued by public companies may be misleading owing to the non-disclosure of methods which distort the results. These published balance-sheets do not necessarily show ' a true and correct view of the state of the company's affairs ' interpreted in any literal sense.

5. The statements, although expressed in terms of money, do not usually give effect to the changing value of money. If this has been fluctuating it follows that comparative results between successive accounting periods do not necessarily reflect true economic trends.

These limitations are of considerable importance to managers, investors, bankers, and others making use of the statements.

Let us now seek some of the causes.

This calls for a consideration of—

(1) The nature of the available information from which accountants prepare the statements ; and

(2) The treatment of that information.

NATURE OF ACCOUNTING INFORMATION.

Regarding the nature of the available information, two points may be noted :—

(*a*) All relevant information has not crystallised into historical fact at the date of the statements or during the period of their preparation. For example, goods may be held for sale, but the selling prices are not yet known ; the outcome of partially executed contracts may be problematical ; the extent to which customers' debts will be collected in cash involves estimates.

(*b*) The information may consist of historical fact, but there may be uncertainty as to its interpretation. This will call for the exercise of judgment in reaching decisions regarding its treatment and application. For example, the cost of permanent assets may be known, but the allocation of this cost to successive time periods, or to production units, may be matters of estimate; the allocation of various classes of expenses against units of production may also be a matter of opinion; the distinction between capital and income may be difficult to define, and even if defined may not easily be determined.

Treatment of Accounting Information.

Regarding the treatment of information, the points mentioned above relating to the nature of the information indicate that its treatment gives scope for the exercise of judgment and discretion and demands accounting decisions.

Any situation requiring the exercise of judgment usually implies the application of some principle or group of principles. This is not confined to matters of accounting, but is probably true of all affairs of life. Frequently two or more principles may be involved in reaching a decision or forming an opinion, and these principles may conflict in varying degrees. The treatment of accounting information will therefore depend on the application of principles. What are these principles ?

Accounting Principles.

In accounting literature the word 'principle' often means a widely accepted rule or practice. For example, one finds in text-books that the method of stock valuation "at cost or market price, whichever is the lower," is described as a principle. Our dictionaries, however, give an alternative meaning to this word, and define it as a "fundamental source or truth." Behind all accounting rules or methods or conventions there must lie some basic reasons or sources from which the accepted practice springs. This is the sense in which I propose to examine accounting 'principles.'

1. Conservatism.

One of the most important is the principle of *Conservatism* or *Financial Prudence*. This has a bearing on many of the rules and conventions adopted in preparing accounting statements. For example, in ascertaining the profit over a particular period, it is generally agreed amongst accountants that income should not be anticipated and treated as effective until it is realised, or has reached a stage where realisation is virtually assured. On the other hand, losses and unfavourable events arising in the course of trade are frequently made effective in an accounting period prior to the conclusion of the transactions involving loss. In all asset valuations cost is widely accepted as an upper limit. If market value is higher it is ignored, but if lower it is applied. Where market value cannot be assessed (as in the case of fixed assets in use), the valuation is based on cost reduced by depreciation. Frequently the depreciation policy is governed by conservative estimates. The creation of reserves against contingencies, either specific or general, also springs from this principle.

2. Comparability.

Another basic principle is *Comparability*. The majority of accounting statements are prepared for continuing enterprises. A series of these statements will constitute the financial history of the undertaking. Each set of statements covering a specific period is merely a chapter in the history, and cannot be interpreted except in the light of what has gone before. Many of the people who examine accounting statements are concerned primarily with the likely course of future events, and use past results as one of the finger-posts. This means that comparisons are made between the results of successive periods to ascertain the development or contraction of economic activities and to disclose changes in financial condition. The accounting statements should therefore be prepared with the object of comparability in view.

3. *Consistency.*

This objective will not be attained unless the principle of *Consistency* is also followed. If it is desired to produce figures for a continuing business which are capable of giving comparisons, there should be consistent methods of treatment of information and uniform methods of presentation. For example, the method originally adopted for the depreciation of each asset should, if possible, be maintained throughout the life of the asset; the method of valuation applied to goods in stock should not be varied; the distinction between capital and revenue should be defined and consistently maintained. As regards uniform methods of presentation, the classification of assets, liabilities, income sources and expenses should not be materially altered from period to period. Similarly the description of items should not be varied without comment.

The growing co-operation between separate units in many different trades and industries has increased the pooling of information for a variety of purposes, such as production quotas, wages ascertainment, price fixing, and trade statistics. For some of these purposes accounting information is required. This has encouraged the adoption of consistent methods of ascertainment by all the co-operating units in the particular trade or industry. At present these requirements do not usually extend to balance-sheets or profit statements, so it cannot be said that the principles of comparability and consistency are yet applicable except within the domestic affairs of each separate business. There is, however, standardisation in the form of published accounts in many types of statutory undertakings. For example, railway, gas, water, insurance companies, building, co-operative, and friendly societies are required by law to produce annual accounts in a standard form prescribed for the particular type of undertaking. The statutory regulations regarding accounts do not establish many rules for the treatment of accounting information, and there is considerable variation in the accounting methods adopted by the individual undertakings. Therefore it should not be thought that standardisation of form will give comparability.

4. Acccuracy.

Accuracy is fundamental in all branches of accounting concerned with the recording of fact. For example, it is one of the predominating principles of book-keeping. It must also be maintained in all calculations connected with financial measurements or valuations. Although there is bound to be a loss of precision wherever estimate is involved, this loss should be minimised as far as possible by the accurate ascertainment of facts relevant to the estimate.

5. Timeliness.

Another accounting principle is *Timeliness*.

The more quickly accounting statements are available, the greater is their usefulness in all cases where past information is a factor in determining future policy. This is particularly true of large concerns where the management cannot have an intimate knowledge of the progress of all activities, and must rely on getting essential information by means of accounting and statistical summaries presented at frequent intervals and without such delay as will put the information out of date. The practice of having statements of profit and financial condition prepared at relatively short intervals (for example, each month or each quarter) is increasing. There is also a continuous drive to reduce the time spent in preparing these statements, thus speeding up the availability of essential information. The assistance afforded by book-keeping and other machines is most valuable in this connection.

6. Convenience.

There is also the principle described as *Convenience*.

The financial transactions of many undertakings are voluminous and varied. It is frequently impossible to show the effect of each separate transaction in the main accounting statements. Probably it would not be of advantage to do so, since the classification and summarisation of like items can give a series of pictures more easily interpreted. While accountants in preparing their statements have convenience of interpretation in mind, it may be difficult to determine the degree of condensation which will produce the most satisfactory summary, particularly if the statements are likely to be examined by people not having a common purpose and interest. For example, the type of information required by a shareholder may be different from the information desired by a banker. To overcome these difficulties the same information may be submitted in several forms.

7. *Disclosure.*

There remains the principle of *Disclosure.*

It is axiomatic of any document purporting to be informative that it should disclose all material facts. If this principle is not applied, then truth is hidden. The principle of disclosure is vital to all accounting statements drawn up to supply information, and most accounting statements have this object. It is not always easy to determine what is material, but information relating to the classification and valuation of assets and to the existence of reserves and provisions is generally of prime importance for all purposes, and should be disclosed.

This principle is not applied in the published form of many accounting statements. In public companies material facts are often concealed from the shareholders. The under-statement of assets and profits is perhaps the most common type of concealment. Manipulations having the object of reducing profit variations between successive periods are also practised. Ultra-conservative methods may be applied in good years, while less prudent methods are adopted in lean years. This varying policy is not disclosed, and as a result the business has the appearance of greater stability of earning power than it has in fact.

While the concealment of truth is contrary to sound accounting principles, this practice may continue as long as the final decisions regarding disclosure are not in the hands of accountants.

Conflict of Principle.

I have attempted to state some of the basic principles which influence accounting methods and statements. It is probably true to say that each of these principles is accepted as sound, but it is also true that there may be considerable conflict in their separate application to any given problem. I should like to give one or two examples of these conflicts.

One of the most obvious is that between *Timeliness* and *Accuracy*. Since it is necessary to make decisions on the treatment of financial information which has not yet crystallised into fact, it follows that delay in preparing accounting statements (up to a past date) may allow the unknown facts to be established, and thus give a greater degree of accuracy. Such a practice obviously sacrifices timeliness. For example, it is necessary to place a valuation on goods in stock for the purposes of each profit statement and balance-sheet. If these statements are not completed until the whole of the stock has been realised, the valuation could be determined from a basis of ascertained fact, but the delay may have robbed the statement of much of its usefulness.

There tends to be a continuous conflict between *Conservatism* and *Comparability* in connection with every asset valuation made for balance-sheet purposes. As a result of the conventional link between the profit statement and the balance-sheet (through the operation of double-entry book-keeping) every asset valuation is reflected in the final profit result. The more prudent the valuation of assets, the lower will be the final net profit. The application of conservative methods of valuation can have upsetting effects on the comparability of profit results between successive periods. To bring this out clearly, let us consider the accepted method of valuation of one or two specific types of assets :—

1. *Stock of Goods.*

It is widely accepted that this asset should be valued at " the lower of cost or market price." While there are conflicting views on the exact meaning of ' cost ' or ' market,' there is little doubt regarding the purpose of the rule. The motive is financial prudence. If the unsold stock is likely to yield a profit it is not prudent to anticipate this profit before the goods are sold. In such cases cost is taken as the basis. On the other hand, if the goods are likely to be realised at less than cost owing to falling prices, provision is made for the anticipated shrinkage in value by basing the valuation on market prices. The important point to note is that such a provision is effective in a period prior to the actual sale of the goods. For example, 1938 results include all the sales for that year and also anticipated losses on goods in stock at the year-end to be sold in 1939. The 1938 results do not include losses on 1938 sales in so far as these were anticipated and made effective during the previous year—1937. The application of this rule means that the profits for any period may not relate solely to the events of that period. The rule may exclude events applicable to the period, and include others not applicable. The comparability of the ascertained profit of successive periods is bound to be upset if there is this overlapping and confusion to any varying degree. Experience shows that this overlapping is by no means constant. In times of falling prices and trade depression stocks may be severely written down, whereas during a spell of rising prices no provision may be required. It would appear, therefore, that "the cost or market rule," while giving a conservative valuation for balance-sheet purposes, conflicts with the consistency of profit ascertainment, and thus with comparability. It has been suggested that this conflict might be overcome if profit results were consistently ascertained on a basis of stock valuation at cost, and any provisions required on grounds of prudence to reduce this valuation below cost were separately applied and disclosed.

2. *Fixed Assets.*

A similar conflict between *Conservatism* and *Comparability* is found in the valuation of fixed assets. The basis of valuation which is widely accepted by accountants is acquisition cost reduced by depreciation. The depreciation represents an estimate of the proportion of original cost which has expired through use and obsolescence. It is charged against profits. A conservative policy for asset depreciation may well result in the whole of the original cost of the asset being charged to profit before the asset has reached the end of its useful life. This means that depreciation charges against profits have been excessive, and it also means that for some time during the life of the asset no depreciation will be required. In these circumstances the comparability of profit periods has been upset. The practice of increasing depreciation charges in years of good trade is another example of this conflict between conservatism and comparability.

Conclusion.

I must now attempt to summarise this short analysis. I have stated some of the limitations of balance-sheets and profit statements, and shown that the reasons lie partly in the nature of accounting information and partly in its treatment by accountants. The accounting rules, methods and conventions in common use are based on principles such as conservatism, comparability, consistency, accuracy, timeliness, convenience and disclosure. I have tried to show that a rule based on a single principle may conflict with other principles, and that the application of a principle which is sound for balance-sheet purposes may run counter to principles of importance in profit statements. From this it is evident that in accounting, as in other affairs of life, principles are not always capable of universal application. Their truth may be limited and varied by the circumstances in which they are applied, and by the clashing with opposing principles. It follows that rules and methods based on principles must have the same limitations, and cannot be rigidly applied under all conditions. Standardisation of accounting methods only seems possible, provided (1) the circumstances to which the method will be applied do not vary in essentials ; and (2) there is agreement amongst accountants as to the extent to which conflicting principles are applicable to these circumstances.

You may think that this analysis has emphasised unduly the limitations of accounting, and that more stress might have been laid on positive features. There are two good reasons why it is necessary to appreciate these limitations. In the first place, it is essential to understand that accounting is not an exact science—and never will be, unless the information to be used changes its nature. Many people are still under the impression that accounting has the precision of mathematics, and they assume that profit statements and balance-sheets are infallible. It is in everyone's interest to dispel this false conception, and the stressing of limitations seems an appropriate way to do so. In the second place, it is important for accountants to analyse the limitations of their science, so as to isolate the causes which might be remedied by changes in accounting methods. To this extent the progress of accounting lies in our own hands, and it is only by scientific research and continuous effort to organise accounting thought that development can be achieved.

ACCOUNTANCY MUST LOOK FORWARD.

By H. C. F. HOLGATE.

READERS of this magazine will not need to be told that the profession of accountancy is an important one, and that its science is worthy of the highest study. Nevertheless, we should find it exceedingly difficult to explain away the fact that there is no Chair of Accounting in London University, whose professorial list is remarkable for its expensive diversity in other directions. Considering the high-sounding 'objects' clauses of the various accountancy bodies, we might suggest that attempts be made to endow a Chair of Accounting Theory in the British capital. It is not through any lack of goodwill on the part of the ordinary member of this Institute, that Society or the other Corporation, &c., of accountants and auditors; we can be sure of this by reason of the prompt response to the projected Accounting Research Association. But it is left to those in charge of the Scottish accounting bodies to display that mixture of imagination and common-sense from which emerges the University teaching and practical training so much a factor in creating the prestige enjoyed by the accountant trained in Scotland.

As a whole, the profession is not looking far enough ahead. In recent years some stout-hearted efforts have been effective in showing that there is a wealth of material available should we decide to claim for accountancy a significance proportionate to its real worth to the community. For this purpose the voluntary efforts of a few who can find it convenient to attend the meetings of the University Accounting Research Association are not enough. The profession must be so compacted that it can call upon the best of its constituents in case of need. The direction of its researches must be co-ordinated by the kind of person who can feel himself relieved of the financial necessity of retaining a busy practice—hence our allusion to the foundation of a Chair at London University, which must be followed by other needed foundations of a similar nature where these do not exist.

Having secured for ourselves the appropriate academic leaders comfortably financially independent, let us turn to the work the profession must now undertake. It seems to be clear that we have many unsolved problems—for example: (i) Are we sure that our present work, notably the audits of public companies, give proper assurances to the public? (ii) Do we yet understand the principles by which we should be guided in recommending allocations to depreciation account? (iii) Are we certain that we have examined mechanisation of book-keeping with enough care to be able to commend this or that system to our clients ? (iv) Do we appreciate to the full the impact of changes in the value of money upon the profit and loss account ?

Some of these problems have already been discussed at length, even if no conclusions have been reached, but it is contended by this present writer that there are two defects of organisation that stunt the growth of research, apart from the neglect of academic leadership. These two matters are, first, the absence of a unified profession, and secondly, the insistence upon undemocratic forms of control of the constituent associations of accountants.

Of these, the existence of more than one society of accountants has been the more debated, for there are already many declarations by members of both 'senior' and 'junior' bodies that they favour registration of accountants —a step that would ultimately end in a unified control. That there may be grounds for preserving the titles 'Chartered,' 'Incorporated,' 'Certified,' or what you will, one must be ready to concede, though this of itself does not afford any real reason why registration should be deferred. And it is no more than deferred, for society will not for ever look with favour upon a system which denies State registration of the public's 'watch-dogs.' It would be better for the dignity and prestige of the profession if the demand for registration came from the various associations speaking with one voice.

The lack of democratic representation in the various accounting bodies is less stressed, but equally serious. In two recent amalgamations the principle whereby members of the governing body must be drawn from a selected class was firmly asserted—and it is a bad principle. It is startling to find that whereas accountants 'not in practice' constitute an overwhelming majority of an association, not one member in this class may sit on the Council. This absurdity has never been explained satisfactorily and cannot be supported or justified.

One does not need to be in practice to understand accounting principles; the practising accountant who accepts a post as a paid employee or director, and gives up his private practice, is none the less capable of directing the affairs of a professional society; specialist fields of accounting are, in the nature of things, more likely to be fully explored by non-practising members, and it is to their text-books that the profession will fly for guidance. Why should the author of, say, 'Rating and Valuation in the Gas Industry' be unqualified to assist in the management of his association even if (as it so happens) he is a 'non-practising' member ? He is not the only specialist author of a standard text-book who is deemed unfit for the democratic right (established in the first place by Britons) of having a say in the use of the money payment levied upon him.

If we are to look forward it must be to the reconsideration of present practices, with a view to extending our usefulness to society. This demands that we shall make the best of the material we have in order to produce a higher standard of competency. Standards must be established that are comprehensible to the public who are ultimately to benefit therefrom. *Ad hoc* inquiries must be undertaken with a view to ensuring that the profession is aware of the true worth of the tools it is offered. Where the profession discovers loopholes in the legislation surrounding business or fiscal accounting arrangements, it must assert itself to demand the appropriate reforms. The public must be protected by a State register of accountants in whom it will come to trust, and whilst this enhancement of the profession of auditing is desirable, the claims of other accountants to a full share in the control of the profession of accounting and auditing must not be brushed aside.

TAX AVOIDANCE.

By T. ROBINSON.

TAX avoidance or evasion is by no means a new subject, and no doubt has been practised in some shape or form since income tax was first imposed. It is, however, only natural that it has come into greater prominence in recent years, due to the heavy increase in income tax and the introduction of N.D.C. and E.P.T., and the question arises : Does the fact of our being engaged in war make avoidance or evasion a bigger 'sin' than in more normal times?

We are not concerned with fraudulent avoidance: there is no question as to how this should be treated, and no powers which the Revenue have can be too strong for such fraud.

The purpose of this article is to draw attention to the unsatisfactory position which exists regarding what can be termed 'legal avoidance.' Now the latter is a very wide term, and embraces all schemes from the simplest arrangements to the most complex, and there is really no limit as to what can be included. For example, take the case of a man who withdraws £375 from the Post Office Savings Bank and with it buys 500 National Savings Certificates, or the man who arranges to get married on 6th April but who is advised that it would be better to make it 5th April, or again he who, after making a voluntary allowance for many years, turns to a deed of covenant for the requisite period of seven years. (Similar simple avoidance schemes can be frustrated for E.P.T. purposes if their main purpose is to reduce the liability—see sec. 35, Finance Act, 1941 ; but as yet there is no power to prevent the three simple schemes mentioned—or others of like nature—reducing liability under, say, Schedule E. or D.) Many more instances could be quoted, but we will conclude our examples with mention of the complex arrangements specially designed by 'experts' where the tax involved is not a matter of a few pounds, but may involve considerable sums—such an arrangement being the well-known recent whisky deals.

In framing a taxing act the Revenue aim at bringing certain specified income into the tax net, and, no matter how much hardship is caused, if the income of any person is caught within the mesh he must pay up—income tax and equity being strangers. Income outside the scope of the Acts is not taxable, and if a taxpayer can convert a taxable source into a non-taxable one in a legal manner, then any tax which would have been payable may be avoided. Can the Revenue quibble at such avoidance ? They stand by the Acts if to their benefit, but let someone find a loophole and immediately the Revenue jump to attention, and if it is worth while a subsequent Act remedies the oversight, and so on *ad infinitum*. No sensible person can possibly quarrel with this; but what has caused considerable annoyance in recent years is the Revenue's practice of discovering that a loophole or a wide-open door has been left, and then not only closing it effectively but also recovering all that has been gained by the taxpayer, by giving to the amendment a retrospective effect.

It is not the writer's intention to take sides in this matter, but merely to draw attention to some pronouncements on the subject, and to suggest that there be some more satisfactory and, if possible, final statement on the whole question.

When legal evasion is practised the ' culprit ' explains away his uneasiness (if he has any) by saying judicial dicta well supports him in his efforts to keep as much as possible of his income for his own use. That there is no doubt whatever that he is well supported will be apparent from the following extracts taken from some of the statements which have been made in the Courts:—

" People are not bound to continue in the same condition of things, either as regards their direct or indirect taxation, which will render either the consumption of articles in the one case, or the property they have in the other, always liable to tax."—Lord Halsbury in *Bullivant* v. *Attorney General*.

" The highest authorities have always recognised that the subject is entitled so to arrange his affairs as not to attract taxes enforced by the Crown so far as he can legitimately do so within the law."— Lord Sumner in *C.I.R.* v. *Fisher's Executors*, 10 T.C. 302.

" No man in this country is under the smallest obligation, moral or other, so to arrange his legal relations to his business or to his property as to enable the Inland Revenue to put the largest possible shovel into his stores. The Inland Revenue is not slow—and quite rightly—to take every advantage which is open to it under the taxing statutes for the purpose of depleting the taxpayer's pocket, and the taxpayer is in like manner entitled to be astute to prevent, so far as he honestly can, the depletion of his means by the Revenue."—Lord Clyde in *Ayrshire Pullman Motor Services* v. *C.I.R.*, 14 T.C. 754.

" It is trite law that His Majesty's subjects are free, if they can, to make their own arrangements so that their cases may fall outside the scope of the taxing Acts. They incur no legal penalties, and, strictly speaking, no moral censure if, having considered the lines drawn by the legislature for the imposition of taxes, they make it their business to walk outside them."—Lord Sumner in *Levene* v. *C.I.R.*, 13 T.C. 486.

From these quotations there can be little doubt that up to recent times a taxpayer was able to argue that any scheme of his for tax avoidance could be justified on both moral and legal grounds—" not the smallest obligation —moral or other."

The majority of taxpayers, however, were prepared to pay their dues, after the usual grumbles; but there were others who, with the heavier rates of tax, tried to take their affairs outside the scope of the taxing Acts by means of schemes—elaborate or otherwise. Even before the war attempts had been made to close certain loopholes, examples of which were the surtax charges on private companies and the attacks made on transfers of assets and voluntary dispositions in several Finance Acts.

At the beginning of the war, however, the whole question probably reached its climax, and one school of thought considered that no further attempts at tax avoidance should be made during the emergency whilst the other still looked upon the Revenue as fair game.

Only quite recently one of the nobility wrote to 'The Times' as follows :—

"Few would say that either our expenditure or our rate of income tax would be the same if it had been necessary to obtain for national finance the consent of an assembly elected only by income taxpayers. Is there in essence much difference between a Hampden refusing to pay ship money and a taxpayer who avoids income tax which has been imposed by a majority who do not pay it themselves? Except indeed that the tax avoider has the Courts of Law on his side, while Hampden had them, however mistakenly, against him. All taxation which does not rest on consent is oppressive; and is it not a good thing that there should be this last lawful remedy against oppressive taxation by a majority that human ingenuity can always find a way by which the minority can escape from tyrannical impost."

Well, the minority can still escape, in some cases, from 'tyrannical impost,' but theirs is now an uneasy escape, because always at the back of their minds must be the thought that in the next or a later Finance Act, their scheme may be brought to nought through a retrospective clause. Suicides have been reported as a result of such legislation.

The dicta of judges serve a useful purpose, but it can be made worthless by a Finance Act (*e.g.*, sec. 35, Finance Act, 1941, which gives power to attack schemes for E.P.T. avoidance whether made before or after the passing of the Act), and tax dodgers have had fair warning from the Chancellor of the Exchequer that he will take all necessary steps to defeat them. So recently as 10th November 1942, in reply to a question on the whisky racket, he said :—

"The Revenue authorities already possess certain powers to deal with tax avoidance, but I should like to give a warning to all concerned that if further powers prove necessary in relation to these or any other schemes of tax avoidance, I shall ask Parliament to grant them, and to grant them with retrospective effect and in such form as to ensure that all the various persons who may have benefited by the transactions will have to pay their share of any tax that may have been lost to the Revenue."

That this was no empty threat is seen by the introduction of sec. 24, Finance Act, 1943 (and the Chancellor's statement on the third reading of the Finance Bill), which raised such a storm in Parliament. It is directed against the avoidance of excess profits tax by disposing of trading stock, under certain conditions, at a price under its market value, and it is retrospective for all E.P.T. purposes; and furthermore, accountants, solicitors, &c., who have made any dealings with the scheme other than for normal fees may be dragged in to liability.

About eighteen months ago the Master of the Rolls also adopted an attitude somewhat different from that expressed in the dicta previously quoted when he said :—

" It would not shock us in the least to find that the legislature had determined to put an end to the struggle by imposing the severest of penalties. It scarcely lies in the mouth of the taxpayer who plays with fire to complain of burnt fingers."

There is also the opinion of the Lord Chancellor as quoted in this magazine for March 1943.

In conclusion, it can be said that past dicta are just a memory, retrospective legislation a present and future threat, and any tax avoiders should realise quite clearly that what is legal to-day may be caught out to-morrow —whether rightly or wrongly we will not argue. Despite the threats, however, all evasion schemes can hardly be covered, and some will escape, especially if the loss of tax is not too high.

Some guidance, however, is needed on what the Revenue regard as unjustified avoidance and avoidance to which they will raise no objection; but such help is not likely to be forthcoming, and evaders must stew in their own juice until such time as the Chancellor considers their scheme worthy of correction.

Caveat emptor in its more modern form could be, " Let the tax avoider beware."

The Accountants' Magazine.

VOL. L.   JUNE 1946.   No. 496

The Editor will be pleased to receive contributions on subjects of interest. Papers which may not be deemed suitable will be returned if desired. Income Tax and other queries will be answered free of charge. The right is reserved to publish any query and reply which is considered of general interest. All Editorial communications should be sent to 23 Rutland Square, Edinburgh.

Public Ownership for the Steel Industry.

THE tendency for the Government to treat the House of Commons with contempt continues to grow. So far as its own supporters are concerned, it would appear that they are expected to approve, without comment, the measures put forward by the Government. And as for the Opposition, they, having lost the Election, are apparently not entitled to question any of the Government's actions. Never was this contempt for Parliament more in evidence than on the occasion of the announcement to apply the principle of public ownership to the steel industry. The peremptory manner in which the decision was conveyed to Parliament is a negation of the democratic principles on which the normal procedure of the House is built. Usually, in the case of a highly technical, important, and controversial matter such as the one in question, a Government would be at great pains to collect and assimilate all the available evidence before putting forward its own policy. At the same time, it would provide the fullest opportunity for public debate, and it would allow the electorate to express its opinion in specific rather than in general terms. Neither of these two conditions have been fulfilled. So far as is known, the Government has rejected the only technical advice it has taken. The seven-year plan submitted to the Minister of Supply was not published prior to the decision. We now know that the report of the Iron and Steel Federation proposes the expenditure of £168 millions over seven years to obtain the highest possible pitch of efficiency. The proposals envisage the increase in the steel capacity of the country from 13¼ million to 16 million tons annually by the developments of big new projects in Scotland, South Wales, and the North-East Coast area, large additions to open-hearth steel capacity in the Midlands, the rebuilding of more than one-third of the existing blast furnaces, and the mechanisation of iron foundries. Proposals of such magnitude surely deserved a thorough public investigation before being cast aside. By their refusal to give information or answer questions when their decision was announced, the Government fully deserved the comment made by Mr Churchill that they were, in effect, giving a decision now and seeking reasons to justify this decision during the next year or so.

The Government's plan to bring the steel industry into public owner-

ship is so vague and shadowy that it is impossible to offer detailed criticism.*
So far as can be seen, a Control Board is to be set up whose task it will be to advise the Minister on nationalisation and to facilitate the execution of urgent schemes of development and modernisation pending the complete transfer of the industry to public ownership. Presumably, too, the Government intend to purchase the property of the steel industry for Government Stock and to put it under the control of a National Steel Board. If this is so, the precedent set in the case of the Coal Bill is being followed, but the definition of the steel industry has still to be worked out.

Centralised control of any industry by a Board, depending on policy decisions made by one Government department, but subject to direction on finance matters by the Treasury, starts life with obvious disadvantages. Administration tends to be slow and cumbrous, and the rigidity and lack of imagination on the part of the Treasury is well known. Even so, public ownership in certain cases might provide more than compensating advantages. The coal industry is a possible example. Public funds, apart, the capital needed to reorganise the industry would probably not be forthcoming, and relations between owners and workers are such that output is seriously impeded. But neither of these two conditions apply to the steel industry. The Iron and Steel Federation have prepared a scheme for the reorganisation of the entire productive capacity of the country, and no difficulties about the availability of capital exist. Harmony between managements, owners, and workers exists to a higher degree in the iron and steel trades than in any other large industry. Exports are rising, and conditions within the industry very healthy. Why then throw the whole position into the melting pot?

But beyond the disadvantages caused by the uncertainty of the future position of the industry, centralised control could well be disastrous for such an industry as that of iron and steel, where diversity is the keynote of the whole organisation. The units in the industry are far from homogeneous, and day-to-day organisation is much more than a matter of routine. Orders received may be large or small; they may be for steels of widely differing carbon content or alloy steels of very different composition. The wide variety of product and size of order require different raw materials and variations in the productive process. And, of course, the finished product, though it may be classed as steel, can take a very wide range of forms. Such variety and diversity need individual management in a large number of operative units, not centralised control in one huge undertaking.

It is likely that the Government will argue that the industry is not sufficiently integrated and that the separation, say, of the blast furnace and steel plant lead to waste of productive effort in solidifying the pig iron, transporting it to the steel furnace and reheating. So much may be granted, but the Federation's plans make adequate allowance for this and suggest a higher degree of integration. If the Government is determined on public ownership, then the solution ought not to be an industry controlled centrally by a National Steel Board, but a number of well integrated and highly equipped companies, each with a very large measure of freedom and independence.

BUDGETARY CONTROL AND STANDARD COSTS.

By ROBERT TAYLOR, C.A.

In the course of the last twenty years there has been developed, in America more than in Britain, a new managerial device known as budgetary control. Professional accountants and accountants in commerce and industry are on the whole unaware of the latest developments in this particular technique and of the advantages to be derived and the economies to be gained therefrom. This article has been written with the purpose of describing briefly the nature of budgetary control and some of the general principles governing its application and operation; it does not attempt to describe in detail how a complete system can be installed or operated.

Until the present technique of combining budgetary control and standard costs was developed, a detailed comparison of current costs with those of previous periods was necessary in order to review operating costs. This was normally done after the lapse of a considerable interval of time, during which occurred losses which could have been avoided had a method been available for accurately measuring the results of current operations. The fundamental features of a system of budgetary control and standard costs are that standards are set for all functions of a business; actual results are rapidly compared with these standards; and by the application of the principle of exception any variation from standard is immediately disclosed and explained. The principle of exception can be defined as the method of presenting accounting and other information on operations and costs in such a way that results which conform to predetermined standards are eliminated, and only variances from standard are brought out, thereby focussing attention on those features which require examination. Consequently, as long as management is satisfied that the standards which have been set are reasonable and represent the best possible level of attainment, attention can be concentrated only on those features which show departures from standard, and which represent avoidable losses or hitherto unforeseen sources of profit.

DEFINITIONS.

A certain amount of confusion exists as to the precise meaning of budgets, standards, standard costs, and budgetary control.

Budgets are estimates or forecasts of sales and of the manufacturing, selling, and distributing expenses thereof. In setting up budgets, standards of cost and efficiency are utilised. Standards imply scientific specifications for quantity and quality of materials and highly efficient manufacturing methods and speeds. They also imply an estimate of the prices to be paid for raw materials and the predetermination of each item of direct and indirect expenses.

Standard costs are estimated costs based on the budgeted level of production and on the predetermined standards of material usage, manufacturing efficiency, prices, wage rates, &c.

Budgetary control is the frequent comparison of actual sales and operating costs with budgeted sales and standard costs, and explanations of any deviations therefrom.

Scope.

It is essential that all activities of a business—selling, manufacturing, and financial—be included and co-ordinated in a scheme of budgetary control. It would be useless, for instance, if the Sales Division set a budget for sales which the Manufacturing Division could not meet; it might be disastrous for the latter to base their budgets and their costs on a production which the Sales Division could not sell. Finally, if sales are rising, it is essential that there is sufficient money available to finance operations, as in most instances increased output necessitates an increase in working capital. Financial budgeting, which involves, *inter alia*, the preparation of budgets of receipts and expenditure, and the balancing of the one with the other in order to control the liquid position of the organisation, is not covered in this article.

Sales Budget.

As the sales budget acts as the foundation on which all other budgets are based, it is of importance that this should be set with great care. It is impossible to assess exactly the volume of future sales, but a careful study of the past results, business trends, and market possibilities is essential if a satisfactory estimate is to be made. In the majority of cases a detailed analysis of sales in preceding years will form the best basis for the budget. This should be analysed over selling lines, territories, and individual salesmen. Graphs showing monthly and moving annual totals of sales for a number of years will assist in the interpretation of sales statistics by indicating general trends and seasonal and cyclical movements. A comparison of these graphs with graphs of business indices or statistics which bear some relation to the particular business may provide a valuable guide to the future. Territorial graphs will indicate trends in sales areas, and graphs of specific lines or groups of products will provide additional valuable information. From these graphs it should be possible to assess the extent to which future sales will vary from the results of previous years.

One method of building up the sales budget is to obtain from the Sales Department a forecast of sales analysed over territories and groups of products. These detailed analyses are considered in relation to market possibilities, and the total sales compared with the estimated trend as shown by the graphs. Should a detailed forecast by the sales organisation be impracticable, an alternative is to fix the total sales of the business, and to break this down to territories and selling lines broadly on the basis of past performance, but having regard to the market possibilities of each district. Whichever method or combination of methods is used, the agreement of the sales personnel that the targets are reasonable should be obtained, as in due course explanations will be required for deviations from budget. In certain industries with a multiplicity of products, and in "special order" and "contract" industries, it is not possible to build up a detailed sales budget over manufacturing lines. In such cases overall percentage increases or decreases of past results have to be applied, but these should be adjusted in any particular group of products or market where special factors which will affect sales are known to exist.

It will be seen later how budgets are established and standard costs obtained for selling, distributing, and manufacturing expenses, and how the net profit, based on the forecasted sales, can accordingly be calculated.

In so far as any variation in the total value of sales affects the profit, the following three factors must be accounted for :—
(1) Variations in volume of sales.
(2) Variations in variety of sales—*i.e.*, in the predetermined ratio of sales of products which bear different margins of profit.
(3) Variations in selling prices.

This can be done by using the following formula :—

Let A = Sales budget.
B = Standard cost of sales budget.
C = Actual sales.
D = Standard cost of actual sales.
E = Value of actual sales at budgeted selling prices.
$F = E \times B/A$ = Standard cost of actual sales at budgeted selling prices (E) if sales had been made in the budgeted variety.

Then the total variation between forecasted standard profit and actual standard profit is $(C-D) - (A-B)$, which can be analysed as follows :—

Variations in selling prices = $C - E$.
Variations in variety = $(E-D) - (E-F)$.
Variations in volume = $(E-F) - (A-B)$.

This analysis of profit should be prepared for each sales area and/or each salesman, and a statement of the variances and the cumulative totals to date should be issued to the Sales Department every month. A statement summarising these results should also be prepared for the benefit of higher management.

EXPENSES.

When preparing budgets for expenses it should be borne in mind that these must be actual estimates of future expenditure and not merely averages of the costs in recent years. Each expense should be separately considered and the general principle adopted that the person responsible for controlling the particular expense should in the first instance submit the budget, and that this in turn should be examined, amended if necessary, and authorised by the management. The budget for each class of expense should be established for varying levels of activity (activity may be defined as the level of actual performance compared with budgeted performance, and is expressed as a percentage of the latter) ; this is done in order to calculate the allowable expenditure in any period in relation to the activity achieved in that period. Thus it is possible to compare actual expenditure with budgeted expenditure, the latter having been adjusted for the volume of activity achieved. Expenses can be classified under three groups :—

(*a*) Fixed.
(*b*) Variable—*i.e.*, varying directly with activity.
(*c*) Semi-variable—*i.e.*, not varying directly with activity but having some relation to it.

It will be found convenient to record the budget for semi-variable expenses at different levels of activity on a graph, with activity along the horizontal axis, and expense on the vertical axis ; in this way it is possible to read off the curve the amount of expense allowable for any level of activity.

The budget for selling and distributing expenses should be analysed over sales areas and the sales-area budgets over products or groups of products. In the case of a large number of expenses it will not be possible to make an accurate allocation, and an arbitrary basis, such as manufacturing cost or weight, will require to be adopted. For each product in each area, a standard cost for selling and distributing expenses can be obtained by dividing the total budgeted expenditure allocated to that product by the estimated quantity of sales. Similarly an overall average standard selling cost can be calculated for each product.

Control of selling and distributing expenses is exercised in the following way :—

Let $A =$ the standard selling and distributing cost of sales at average rates—*i.e.*, quantity of sales $\times$ the overall average standard selling and distributing cost.

$B =$ the standard selling and distributing cost of sales at the rate appropriate to the area in which the sales were made.

$C =$ the allowed cost of sales, as calculated by reference to the activity.

$D =$ Actual expenditure.

Then $A - B =$ the geographical variance, or the variance between the standard cost for the whole business and the standard cost in the particular area.

$B - C =$ the volume variance and represents the under-recovery or over-recovery of fixed expenses due to the volume of sales differing from the budget.

$C - D =$ the expense variance, or the amount by which actual expenditure differs from estimated expenditure adjusted for the actual volume of sales achieved.

$A - D =$ total variance.

This analysis is prepared in the first instance for each sales area, and the results of all areas are summarised in order to give the results of the whole business. The geographical variance should be self-cancelling if the proportion of actual sales in the various sales areas to total sales is in line with the sales budget. In certain industries sales are subject to wide seasonal fluctuations. Allowance can be made for this both in the sales budgets and in the expense budgets, and its effect on the recovery of fixed expenses can be calculated and isolated in the analysis of variances.

Manufacturing Costs.

Principles similar to those used in budgeting and controlling sales and selling and distributing expenses are applied to manufacturing costs. Total manufacturing cost is made up of—

(*a*) The cost of raw materials.
(*b*) Direct labour.
(*c*) Expenses which can be allocated directly either to the product or to a manufacturing section of the factory.
(*d*) Overhead expenses.

Control of materials includes control of cost prices as well as control of the quantities used in production. Price-control is obtained by setting a standard cost price for each material and then comparing actual cost with standard cost as and when material is purchased. Usage-control involves setting standards for the quantity of materials to be used in the production of each product; these are based on scientific, engineering, or other technical specifications, allowance being made for wastage and the recovery of by-products, if any. Standard material costs for each product can be built up from the material specification and the list of standard cost prices. Material-control can be exercised by using the following formula :—

Let A = Cost of materials purchased valued at standard prices.
B = Actual cost of purchases.
C = Standard material-cost of production at standard prices.
D = Actual material-usage at standard prices.
E = Standard quantity of by-products at standard prices.
F = Actual quantity of by-products at standard prices.

Then $A - B$ = the price variance.
$C - D$ = the usage variance.
$F - E$ = the variance due to the non-standard recovery of by-products.

It will be noticed that the price variance is calculated on purchases, whereas the usage and by-products variances are related to production. If considered expedient, the price variance can be calculated as and when materials are used, but it will still remain necessary to produce statements showing variances in purchase prices in order to control the Purchasing Department.

To control labour and other direct and indirect expenses it is necessary to divide the factory into production departments and to subdivide the production departments into cost sections. Generally, production departments will coincide with established lines of supervisory responsibility; cost sections will consist of (1) individual machines or (2) groups of machines, the operating costs of which are equal. In order to predetermine the output of a cost section it is necessary, in view of the multiplicity of products which may be manufactured in that section, to have a common unit of measurement. In the majority of cases the value of production will vary directly with the amount of time spent in achieving that production; the measure of output can accordingly be either a man-hour or a machine-hour, whichever is considered more suitable for the particular factory, and the budget of output for each cost section can be stated in standard hours. In order to assess the level of output, reference will have to be made to the sales budget. In certain factories it may be possible to break this down into standard hours for each cost section; in others it may be found impracticable to do this, in which case a more arbitrary method will have to be employed, such as factoring the hours worked in the previous year by the proportion by which budgeted sales differ from the sales of the previous year, both calculated at the same prices.

Having fixed the budgets for output, it becomes necessary to establish the budgets for labour and other expenses. As in the case of selling and distributing expenses, these budgets should be fixed for all reasonable levels of activity, in order that actual expenditure may be compared in due course with allowable expenditure, having regard to the level of output attained. Once the budgets are fixed, each item of expense is allocated as equitably as possible to the various cost sections; direct labour and direct expenses can be allocated more or less directly to the appropriate cost section. Overhead expenses are allocated in the first instance to production departments and then within each production department to cost sections. In this way, by dividing the total expenses allocated to each cost section by the output of that section as expressed in standard hours, a standard cost rate per hour can be obtained.

The method of building up the standard cost of each product manufactured differs with the type of industry. In " process " industries, to the standard material cost is added the standard manufacturing cost in each process, obtained by multiplying the standard time the product takes in each process by the standard costing rate for that process. In " assembly " industries the standard cost of each component has to be calculated in the first place by adding to the standard material cost the product of the standard time and the appropriate costing rate; then, having calculated the standard cost of all components, it is necessary only to add to the sum of these the standard cost of assembling.

VARIANCES.

In the case of direct labour, direct expenses, and indirect expenses, variances between standard and actual cost can be the result of any of three factors. In the first place, if the level of production differs from the budgeted level, there will be an under- or over-absorption of fixed expenses, as the latter have been included in the costing rates on the basis of budgeted output; this under- or over-recovery is known as the *volume variance*.

Secondly, if the actual speed of output per man-hour or machine-hour is below the standard speed of output, or, to express it differently, if the actual hours worked exceed the output expressed as standard or permissible hours, then there is a loss as compared with standard, as more time and therefore expense has been incurred than was originally considered adequate. Conversely, if the actual speed of output exceeds the standard speed, there is a gain; this gain or loss is known as the *efficiency variance*.

Finally, there is the *expense variance*, which is the result of extravagances or economies in manufacture, such as employing higher or lower grades of labour, using more or less power, &c., than was estimated in the budget.

In order to obtain the standard value of production and to calculate the variances from standard, it is necessary to collect the following information:—

    (i) Output per cost section expressed as standard hours.
    (ii) Actual hours worked per cost section.
    (iii) Actual direct labour costs per cost section.
    (iv) Actual direct expenses per production department.

Then the standard value of production is equal to the output in standard hours of the various cost sections multiplied by the costing rates appropriate to each cost section.

The variances in direct labour costs can be obtained in the following way for each cost section:—

Let A = Output in standard hours multiplied by the direct labour element of the standard costing rate.

B = Actual hours worked multiplied by the same factor—*i.e.*, what the value of production in respect of direct labour would have been if for every hour worked one standard hour had been produced.
C = Actual direct labour costs.
Then A − B = the efficiency variance.
B − C = the expense variance.

It is not practicable to control direct expenses by cost section, as certain expenses, such as supervision and electric light, are of the nature of overhead expenses, while others, such as power, although variable with output, are not usually measured at each cost section, and as a result actual costs thereof per cost section are unobtainable. They can be controlled by manufacturing departments, however, in the following way :—

Let A = Standard direct expenses absorbed—*i.e.*, the product of the output in standard hours and the direct expenses element of the standard costing rate.
B = Allowable expenditure based on an activity calculated as follows :—

$$\frac{\text{Output in standard hours} \times \text{standard costing rate}}{\text{Total departmental budget}}$$

i.e., allowable expenditure on the basis of the actual efficiency achieved.

C = Allowable expenditure based on an activity calculated as follows :—

$$\frac{\text{Actual hours worked} \times \text{standard costing rate}}{\text{Total departmental budget}}$$

i.e., allowable expenditure on the basis that manufacturing efficiency has been 100 per cent.

D = Actual expenditure.
Then A − D = total variance.
A − B = the volume variance.
B − C = the efficiency variance.
C − D = the expense variance.

General factory overhead expenses are controlled in the same way as direct expenses are controlled for a production department, and by using similar principles it is possible to calculate the volume, efficiency, and expense variances on this group of expenses. As with selling and distributing expenses in those industries which show wide seasonal fluctuations in output, the effect of varying levels of activity on the recovery of fixed overhead expenses can be calculated and shown as a seasonal variance, which in the course of the year should be self-cancelling.

PERIODICAL PROFIT AND LOSS REPORT.

From the foregoing it will be seen that it is possible to prepare every month a statement on the lines of the accompanying illustration. This statement should be supported by subsidiary statements, in which are shown detailed analyses of the variances over selling lines, sales areas, salesmen, manufacturing departments, &c. From these it is claimed that management can obtain a clear picture of the operation of its organisation: the effect on profits of any variations from standards is isolated and evaluated, and attention need be directed only to those factors which are causing wide variances.

On the question of the cost of operating a system of budgetary control and standard costs, it may be stated that in the majority of cases, as far as accounting staff are concerned, such a system is more economical to operate than any system of detailed actual costs. On the other hand, especially in its initial stages, it involves an examination by management of all standards of efficiency and budgets of expenditure. Although this may be a fairly onerous task, one immediate advantage is that an investigation is made of all phases of an organisation, some of which are liable to be overlooked, thus leaving undetected concealed sources of waste.

In conclusion, it may be said that budgetary control cannot take the place of effective management; it is only a device which draws the attention of management to the source of avoidable losses, thus freeing it of the necessity to be continually investigating all phases of an organisation and allowing it to concentrate its energies on those features only which show marked departures from predetermined standards of selling and operating efficiency and cost.

PROFIT AND LOSS REPORT FOR MONTH OF DECEMBER 1946.

(Deductions shown in italics would in practice be shown in colour.)

Budgeted profit			£23,000
Sales variances—			
(a) Selling prices	£2000		
(b) Variety of sales	*500*		
(c) Volume of sales	3500		
		5,000	
Actual standard profit			£28,000
Selling and distributing expense variances—			
(a) Geographical	£200		
(b) Volume	750		
(c) Expense	*250*		
	£300		
Manufacturing variances—			
(1) Materials—			
(a) Cost	£2000		
(b) Usage	750		
(c) By-products	*300*		
	£950		
(2) Direct labour—			
(a) Efficiency	£500		
(b) Cost	*200*		
	300		
Carry forward	£1250	£300	£28,000

Brought forward .		£1,250	£300	£28,000

(3) Direct expenses—
    (a) Volume £300
    (b) Efficiency *350*
    (c) Expense 150
                                                       100

(4) Overhead expenses—
    (a) Volume £400
    (b) Efficiency *650*
    (c) Expense 200
                                                       450
                                                                1600
                                                                             1,300

Actual trading profit £26,700
Special receipts or expenditure not included in standard costs . 800

Actual profit £27,500

Note.—Cumulative figures to date to be shown in column on right of the above statement.

The Effects of the Price Level on Accounting*
By F. R. M. de PAULA, C.B.E., F.C.A.

WITHOUT doubt, the subject that we have to consider is one that is greatly exercising the minds of accountants throughout the world. This fact was made vividly clear by the papers laid before and the discussions at the Sixth International Congress on Accounting, which took place in London during the past summer. This Congress afforded an ideal opportunity for a full exchange of views upon this vitally important and, at the same time, contentious problem. From these discussions, it is clear that there is a deep cleavage of opinion regarding the fundamental principles of accounting as regards this matter. There are two distinct schools of thought, and they are as opposite as the North Pole is from the South.

This difference of opinion exists both without and within the accountancy profession itself and it would seem to be urgently necessary that the profession should make every effort " to close its ranks." We must, therefore, make up our minds whether we stand firm for orthodoxy, whether we shall embrace the new gospel that is being preached throughout the land or whether there is some other way by which we can solve this vexed problem.

The background of the problem

This question is centred upon the effects on industry of rising prices, together with the ever-increasing burden of taxation. These are the two

---
* A paper delivered on October 10, 1952 in Edinburgh before The Chartered Accountants Students' Society of Edinburgh.

blades of the scissors which cut ever deeper into earnings and thus make it increasingly difficult for both industry and individual members of the community to accumulate savings. In consequence of this adverse trend, which has been gathering great force in recent years, industry is unable to accumulate out of earnings sufficient extra capital to replace, at enhanced costs, its fixed and current assets.

The vital question, therefore, is how the necessary increased capital required is to be provided in order to ensure that our industries can maintain their existing earning capacity.

There have been similar adverse trends in the past, and the additional capital requirements were generally provided for (*a*) out of profits ploughed back into the business and/or (*b*) out of new capital subscribed by members of the community out of their savings. To-day, supplies of capital under both (*a*) and (*b*) are failing, due to the crushing burden of taxation and the great increase in the level of prices. In these circumstances industry is becoming extremely anxious as to how and from what sources its future capital requirements are to be provided. If adequate supplies are not available then our industries must inevitably languish. Thus the National Economy would have received what might prove to be a mortal wound. If our industries failed, the immediate effect must be that we no longer could maintain, in these small islands, our present population of some 50 million persons.

To live we have to import over 50 per cent of our requirements of food and in addition by far the greater part of the raw materials that we need. Exports are the only means by which we can pay for our imports from abroad, which are essential for our continued existence. Our national burden has, in recent years, been made much heavier by reason of the great rise in the level of prices, which has increased the cost of our purchases from abroad. Increasing foreign competition in the export field has accentuated our difficulties.

It is clearly a vital national need that our industries should be developed to their maximum capacity and productivity; therefore, an adequate supply of capital is essential; indeed it may be said that capital is the life blood of industry.

All of us appreciate these facts, and there is a new school of thought that contends that a great part of the necessary future requirements of capital could be provided for by altering our basic accounting methods. From the public discussions upon this problem, one might well form the opinion that a great part of our national troubles would be surmounted if only accountants would mend their ways; but is the solution of these grave difficulties as simple as that?

The new conception of profits

The new conception of profits has been pressed strongly by economists, industrialists and a growing number of accountants, and the objects are to overcome the adverse effects of the rising price level and to reduce the crushing burden of taxation upon industry and commerce; thus blunting the edges of the two blades of the scissors that are cutting so hurtfully into industrial earnings. All accountants will agree with the objects in view, but there is a difference of opinion as to the means suggested for their achievement.

The time-honoured conception of profits or losses has been defined by the Council of The Institute of Chartered Accountants in England and Wales as follows:—

> " Profit or loss on trading is the difference between the amount for which goods are sold and their cost, including the cost of selling and delivery."

That has been the basis throughout the ages and in effect represents counting the money out of and back into the till. Personal opinion is at a minimum in connection with the preparation of accounts upon this basis; it is obvious, however, that accounts prepared upon these principles have many limitations.

The advocates of the new conception of profits or losses discard completely the foregoing simple basis, and contend that profits and losses should be measured by evaluation, broadly as follows:—

(a) Expired capital outlay upon fixed assets should be charged against revenue upon the basis of the estimated cost of replacement of such assets.

(b) Inventories consumed should be charged against sales proceeds at the estimated cost of replacing them instead of at their original cost.

Thus, it is contended, correct adjustment would be made for variations in the purchasing power of the monetary unit.

If this new conception were accepted and were drafted into our Company law, as would seem to be necessary, then these alterations in the fundamental bases of accounting would represent a complete revolution. The accountancy profession, in effect, would, thereby, admit that in the past:—

(a) Accounts had been prepared upon a completely incorrect basis.

(b) In times of rising prices, the error factor might have been very considerable.

(c) Serious overpayments of dividend might have been made to shareholders.
(d) Funds available for the payment of creditors might have been seriously depleted.
(e) Earnings shown in past prospectuses might have been grossly overstated and thus have misled subscribers.

It would seem that, for these and many other reasons, the accountancy profession would be most unwise to make so drastic and fundamental a change in its basic principles, unless and until it was convinced beyond any question of doubt that the new conception was correct. At the moment the Council of the English Institute, the Council of the American Institute of Accountants and many of the general body of accountants are very doubtful indeed both as regards the soundness of and practicability of the new conception of profits or losses. The Council of the English Institute has suggested that there should be further discussions and considerations of this whole question by all of the accountancy bodies in this country. This would seem to be eminently wise upon the maxim that we should look carefully before we leap.

Taxation

The advocates of the new conception contend that it should be applied to the calculation of profits or losses for taxation purposes. Thus the tax burden upon industry and commerce would be very substantially reduced. This contention has been pressed upon the Inland Revenue in recent years, but so far has not been accepted. This perhaps is not surprising, as the accountancy profession itself has not yet made up its mind upon this important point.

If the new conception were accepted by the Inland Revenue, the benefit to industry and commerce would be very great indeed. Important questions would arise—for example, how and by whom the consequent loss of Government tax revenue should be borne, and what would be the reactions of all other taxpayers who were not granted similar benefits. So long as the Inland Revenue maintains its present stand, then any amounts set aside by industry towards the enhanced cost of replacement of fixed and current assets must be provided out of taxed income. Thus the funds available for this purpose would be greatly constricted.

The practical application of the new conception of profits

The Council of the English Institute has carefully considered this whole problem in its " Recommendations on Accounting Principles," Nos. IX, X, XII and XV. These I strongly advise you to study, if you wish to understand why the Council of the English Institute is unable to accept any of the various schemes that have been put forward to date. Many of you may not agree with the conclusions contained in these recommendations.

The fact that the English Institute, the American Institute of Accountants and many of the general body of accountants have not been able to accept the new conception of profits is a most important factor, as progress would be very difficult and slow without unanimity within the profession. Each side, therefore, must try to understand fully the views of the other, so that they may come to mutual agreement. May it not be that the " middle of the road " may lead to the desired goal?

Some points for consideration

The following are a few points in connection with this matter that need consideration:—

(1) One of the objections to the historical cost conception is that, under it, the balance sheet items are stated in monetary units of different purchasing values. Under the new conception, if current value were applied only to fixed and current assets and not to all of the other items, would not that balance sheet also be in monetary units of different purchasing values?

(2) Is not one of the stumbling blocks, in the way of general agreement, that many do not agree with the English Institute that " any amount set aside to finance replacements (whether of fixed or current assets) at enhanced costs should not be treated as a provision which must be made before profit for the year can be ascertained, but as a transfer to reserve "? Legal opinion seems to endorse this view. This is a fundamental point which must be settled, if progress is to be made towards general agreement. If the English Institute's opinion on this point were accepted, then many of the difficulties would, I suggest, disappear.

(3) The maximum amount that can be set aside out of revenue, to finance replacement of assets at enhanced costs, is 100 per cent of the surplus of earnings of an undertaking, calculated on the historical cost basis. Might not the full application of the new conception of profits result, in many cases, in the creation of an impossible burden for a company to bear? If so, might not the interests of shareholders, and other parties concerned, be gravely prejudiced?

(4) If full provision were made for the enhanced cost of replacements of fixed and current assets, and these provisions were added into costs for price-fixing purposes, might not this accelerate the inflationary spiral and possibly result in a " buyers' strike "?
(5) As, during the lifetime of an asset, current values might be fluctuating between wide limits, would it not be impossible to achieve fair annual distribution of the total cost of replacement, over the whole of the asset's life?
(6) In the case of an old company, with considerable amounts invested in fixed assets, would it not often be impossible to provide in full for the under-provisions in the years prior to the adoption of the new conception for calculating profits?
(7) In view of the fact that it is impossible to estimate accurately the future cost of replacing an asset, does not that mean that it is impossible accurately to calculate the ultimate amount of capital required?
(8) Would not the application of the new conception necessitate a maximum amount of personal opinion in the making of the annual evaluations?
(9) Would not great difficulties arise in connection with the audit of accounts prepared upon the basis of the new conception?
(10) How would the Inland Revenue be able to verify accounts prepared upon the basis of the new conception?

A growing practice has developed of allocating lump sums from available profits to Capital Reserve, towards the finance required for the replacement of assets at enhanced costs. Pending the settlement of this vexed problem, is not this the most simple and practical method for dealing with this matter? This is in line with the views of the Council of the English Institute, which, as I understand them, are that the setting aside of such amounts is a matter of financial policy and that such amounts are not compulsory charges against earnings.

If the above were accepted, then auditors would not be concerned with the creation of any such reserves, and these matters would be the responsibility of the board of directors.

Conclusion

In the circumstances of to-day, when industry is facing the possibilities of an acute shortage of capital brought about as the result of inflation and heavy taxation, it is obviously wise and prudent that the boards of companies should make these facts as clear as possible to shareholders and others concerned. The accounts themselves, the directors' report and the chairman's statement are all available for this purpose.

Ultimately the whole basis of accounting may be altered in line with a new conception of profits, but that time has not yet arrived. In the meantime it is hoped that, as the result of full discussion, the right solution of this complicated and contentious problem will be found.

The accounts of companies are used for many different purposes and the purpose for which the figures are required governs the accepted conventions upon which they are based. The published accounts of a company in this country are drawn up in accordance with the provisions of the Companies Act and the regulations of that company. Such accounts are founded upon an accepted code of conventions and cannot serve all the various purposes for which accounts are required. There cannot be such a thing as an " all purpose " balance sheet and profit and loss account.

May not the possible solution of our problem be upon the lines of presenting the legal accounts with the accompaniment of supplementary statements and figures? One of such statements might well be a detailed calculation of the estimated extra capital required in the future to finance the enhanced cost of replacement of fixed and current assets. Particulars might also be given of the exact extent to which provision had in fact been made, for this contingency, in the legal accounts. Might not such a procedure overcome many of the difficulties that are preventing general agreement within our profession?

The root cause of these difficulties

Mr Edward B. Wilcox, C.P.A., in his brilliant paper at the recent Congress, concluded with the significant and thought-provoking remark, that " It should be borne in mind, however, that the trouble lies in inflation itself, and that prevention of inflation would not only eliminate the accounting problems which result from it, but would also be of greater social usefulness than any conceivable adjustment of accounts."

This statement, in my opinion, goes to the root of the problem that we are considering. May it not represent the key?

Are not the financial and accounting troubles and difficulties merely the symptoms of a fell disease, deeply seated in our National Economy?

May it be that we accountants are concentrating on applying palliatives to those symptoms, whereas no cure can be effected except by attacking the deep-seated cancer? Is not Mr Wilcox correct, when he points out to us that, in this case, that deep-seated cancer is inflation?

If Mr Wilcox is correct, then the alteration of our accounting principles will not effect the complete cure that we all are searching for. The problem is, therefore, a political one, and one of vital importance to the whole nation.

The tide of inflation sweeps over all, none can escape its effects—industry, commerce and every individual citizen. As regards industry, the inevitable effect is the draining away of available capital, owing to the reducing purchasing power of the monetary unit.

Is not this country living in "a fool's paradise"? Are we not refusing to face the grim facts, that we are no longer a rich nation and are not, therefore, able to maintain our old standards of life?

Is not the only hope for us to put our national house in order, by ruthlessly cutting down our national expenditure to balance our income? That would entail many sacrifices. On the other hand we would need to make every endeavour to increase our national productivity to the maximum.

If this statement is correct, then no alteration of our accounting principles will eradicate the root cause of the problem that we have been considering.

Summer School Impressions

By A MEMBER

THE first pre-requisite to the success of any serious, single-minded summer school or conference is to hold it in a place which offers as many distractions as possible. There is no need, therefore, to enquire too closely into how many members came to the first summer school of the Institute primarily to discuss professional problems and how many came principally to renew acquaintance with St Andrews. Certainly to those members of the school who knew of old its subtle charm—and they seem to be much in the majority—the answer to such a question was completely unambiguous.

The school assembled officially on Friday afternoon, although two members who had travelled overnight from London were observed making a preliminary reconnaissance round on the Old Course as early as ten o'clock on the morning of that day. Members in commerce appeared, generally, to arrive in slightly grander state than their colleagues in practice, but the absence of porters and lifts in St Salvator's Hall, which reduced everyone to being his own *sherpa*, tended to make an overabundance of baggage a liability rather than an asset. After the simple formalities of registration were over and rooms—commodious 'bedsitters'—had been claimed, tea was served in the Dining Hall. Here members indulged in the game of spotting celebrities. These were of two kinds—the illustrious past of the university whose likenesses, in oils or in stained glass, looked down from the high walls and windows upon the assembly; and the illustrious present of the profession, three-dimensional and easily recognisable by the name badges pinned on their lapels. One member, it was noticed, wore his badge upside down, presumably either the more easily to identify himself by a downward glance or in an attempt to preserve his anonymity and yet comply with the rules.

The remainder of the first day was devoted to "settling in." An excellent lecture on St Andrews, illustrated by lantern slides, was given by Professor John Read, sherry was dispensed in the Common Room, and at dinner afterwards, the Vice-Chancellor extended a gracious welcome to those taking part in the course. The only other scheduled event of the evening was a short meeting of each of the nine discussion groups to plan the programme ahead. These preliminaries set the stage for the four days' intensive work which followed.

The routine of the course soon became familiar, the sequence being breakfast, lecture, coffee, group discussion, lunch, afternoon free, dinner, plenary discussion, a walk and so to bed. For three out of the four days this was the recognised pattern. The exception was Sunday when a morning service was held in the ancient chapel of St Salvator and lectures and discussions, interspersed with meals, went on continuously from lunch until bedtime. It should perhaps be noted that, on the previous evening, a motion by a small subversive element who thought that members were being worked too hard and that the Sabbath programme should be eased was overwhelmingly defeated. This minor and mannerly rebellion may, or may not, have been prompted by an extra in the form of an address on monetary policy by Mr Archibald Campbell of Glasgow University. His discourse was eloquent and profound but, coming as it did immediately after dinner, was unofficially but not inaptly described by one member, replete and momentarily unreceptive to further wisdom, as a little heavy relief.

The morning lectures were given in the Arts Lecture Room, the benches of which were built for concentration rather than for comfort. It was in this room that each of the lecturers, after being introduced by Professor Browning, the permanent chairman at all the plenary sessions, had first to face the school. These morning sessions, with everyone mentally fresh, were perhaps the most enjoyable of the day. Each lasted an hour and a half and while it had originally been intended that the papers should be summarised in that time, what did in fact happen was that each lecturer amplified his written observations and indicated the pointers for subsequent discussion. A distinct technique, inspired by the first lecturer, Mr Dowling, and employed with equal wit and distinction by all the others, was soon evolved. The opening gambit was to talk first for a few minutes without any reference to the particular subject or, indeed, to accountancy at all. Then, veering round gradually to the matter on hand (" If any of you have read as far as the middle of the first page of my lecture . . ." was Mr Hutton's way of getting down to brass tacks), a brilliant expository talk was unleashed on the audience, now happily attuned, punctuated with a number of penetrating questions, of the answers to which the lecturer would disarmingly deny all knowledge.

Coffee was taken around eleven in the ancient house of the Admirable Crichton, now used as the Men Students' Union. Thereafter, the school split up into its respective discussion groups and, for another hour and a half until lunch-time, pulled the particular paper under fire to pieces and then refashioned it according to the majority views of the group members. These meetings, which were held in the Class Libraries in United College Buildings, called for considerable tact on the part of the group leaders. They had to keep a tight rein on the flow of talk, separating the objective from the subjective in comment and criticism (it was noticeable throughout all the discussions that members tended to the particular rather than to the general), ensuring that the meeting did not stray to point four when it was still supposed to be discussing point one and generally canalising thought to some finite conclusions. It is a tribute to the capabilities of the group leaders that lunch-time arrived too precipitately at nearly every session. There was certainly no time for a stroll and a leisurely aperitif beforehand. Those with midday thirsts to quench had to draw on their stocks of beer tickets which could be transmuted in the Dining Hall into the amber and old gold of Messrs Younger's selected ales.

The afternoon's leisure was spent in a number of ways, nearly all of them connected with golf, which was not surprising in a city which, according to R. F. Murray, the St Andrews University poet, is given over, soul and body, to the tyrannising game. Some renegades went to Carnoustie on Monday or Tuesday to watch the first days of the Open Championship, but most of the members disported themselves after their own fashion nearer home on the Elysian Fields, as part of the terrain of the St Andrews courses is aptly named. The weather reserved its worst for Sunday so that, on the other afternoons, the maximum of outdoor recreation was made possible. For this reason, appetites at dinner seemed sharper. Throughout the course, the standard of catering and the excellence of the table service would have done credit to any hotel however many stars it boasted.

The climax of the day came, albeit a little drowsily sometimes, at the evening plenary session in the Common Room when all the tangled skeins of the day's arguments were neatly unravelled. Members grouped themselves informally round the room, these with the smallest appetites getting the first choice of chair, which varied from the deeply luxurious to the stacked metal and canvas kind. At a table beneath one of the tall windows sat the chairman with the lecturer, or lecturers, of the day. The order of procedure for the first evening was that each of the group leaders in turn put the points made by members of their groups and then the lecturer—on this occasion, Mr Dowling—gave his replies and further comments. On the second evening, those who had made observations at group meetings were encouraged to put them directly to the lecturers and, as the ultimate refinement on the last two evenings, each point was made (by the group members) and dealt with (by the lecturers) in succession before proceeding to the next. At each of the four sessions, supplementary comments and questions from the body of the hall were welcomed. Apart from the first evening, when there was a short interval, proceedings were continuous and it was usually long after closing time

(10 p.m.) before the lecturers had stunned their audiences into quiescence. The dialectic standard was of a high order, particularly on the part of the lecturers who had, perforce, to speak impromptu and, in many cases, members speaking from the audience fared much better when they discarded their carefully prepared notes and spoke eloquently from the heart as well as from the head.

The last ritual of the day was for most a walk in the gloaming to the end of the harbour or to the golf links. It was during these meanderings that all the brilliant things left unsaid were remembered but, in the timeless serenity of the silent grey streets which had survived many centuries, the question of replacement values and all the other problems so lately hotly debated ceased, somehow, to have any significance.

This daily cycle, four times repeated, produced a number of mental "snapshots" which keep recurring in the mind. There is the impression, for example, of the members gathering in the picturesque quadrangle preparatory to entering School III. for the morning lecture and again, after coffee, for the discussion group sessions. " THEY canna be students," said one sceptical old holiday-maker to her friend as they watched the multitude assemble. Then there was the discussion group that, taking advantage of a sunny morning, held a meeting on the lawn of St Salvator's Quadrangle. With their chairs forming a complete circle, all the members clutching papers and one of them waving his hands to illustrate the point he was making, they looked, from afar off, like a glee club in session from which, strangely, no sound emanated. Again, there was the picturesque view from the back benches (into which some, conditioned by their schooldays when they got as far away from the master as possible, automatically slid) of the Arts Lecture Room through the windows towards the ancient tower of St Salvator's Chapel, with the green quadrangle in the foreground, a silhouette of some of the oldest of the university buildings beyond and, far above, the wonderful blue sky, banked with white cumulus clouds, so typical of the St Andrews scene. There was the impressive Sunday morning service in the fifteenth-century chapel with the President and the Vice-President reading the lessons and the Professor of Divinity preaching an inspiring sermon from the pulpit reputed to have been used by John Knox. . . . and, to mention only one more of the many memorable scenes, the crowded Common Room at the evening plenary sessions, with the air growing progressively greyer with tobacco smoke, the light slowly draining from the tall windows and, as time went on, the genial smile of Professor Browning becoming ever more the focal point of the whole proceedings.

These are visual recollections. Of a host of other impressions, three qualities which manifested themselves consistently throughout the course must briefly be mentioned. The first is the abundant wit which enlivened the discussions. One of the two ladies attending the school complained to Mr Risk that his operation layout for girls' pyjamas provided only enough cloth per pair for a slim girl of fourteen but enough elastic for an outsize woman. Amid the uproar, Mr Risk was understood to say that the figures would have to be examined more closely else the whole thing might fall to the ground. There was, also, Mr McKellar's candid question to the school, after using the parable of the ten virgins to illustrate an example, as to whether it would rather be in the light with the wise or in the dark with the foolish.

Allied to wit was the quality of high thinking. The only possible complaint which could be made against the fare provided by the lecturers was that the papers contained, almost certainly, too much food for thought. On several occasions discussion groups had some difficulty in digesting it all in the time available for consideration. It happened that, in years, the lecturers were all neatly poised between "crabbed age and youth" and were thus able to appreciate, if not always to agree with, the views of both their elders and their juniors. The older members of the school, as was perhaps to be expected, were generally apathetic towards such comparative innovations as the "one-sided" balance sheet, depreciation being calculated on replacement values rather than on historic cost, and apprentices spending six months in industry as part of their five years' basic training. It was left, in the main, to the younger members—many of them in commerce—to acclaim these developments. The arguments on both sides were delivered with reason, restraint and—the third distinguishing quality of the course—enthusiasm. It was rumoured at the outset that a summer school "in another place" sometimes continued its deliberations until three in the morning, but this inconclusiveness was attributed, scornfully by some, to the inability of its members ever to make up their minds and, wistfully by others, to the apparently greater and later facilities for negotiating beer tickets which existed at Oxford. At St Andrews after dinner, high thinking and plain living were the rule for the rest of the evening. One could drink only at the Pierian spring so that the remarkable level of enthusiasm maintained was not simulated—or stimulated—by anything other than genuine interest in the problems of the profession.

The experiment of taking a representative cross-section of the profession, thoroughly mixing it in an ideal environment, letting it simmer and then watching the emergence of personalities and points of view is over. It has been so successful that it is likely to become an established event and the President indicated that next year's school would be held—at

St Andrews, of course—in late September. By then, a completely new set of professional problems may have to be faced by lecturers and listeners, just as those who learned this year to play the Old Course under summer conditions will have to begin all over again and master it in the mellow, golden afternoons of early autumn. Change is a constant challenge and the prospect, distant though it is, of returning to St Andrews to renew the struggle is exhilarating.

Interpretation of Company Accounts *

By H. E. WINCOTT

THE OBSERVER, that Sunday paper of increasing influence, carries from time to time articles signed by " A Student of Politics." An American visitor to this country is reported to have said, on reading this by-line: " Fancy getting a stoodent to write their articles. Why don't they use a professor? "

I suspect there is an equal danger of misunderstanding where your Society is involved. Although you describe yourselves as students, I have an uneasy feeling that you know more about certain aspects of the subject of my talk than I do. After all, the only contact I have had with accountancy was when, over thirty years ago, I started my business life in the offices of a chartered accountant. It took me just two years to discover that whatever talents I may or may not have, an accountant's office was not the place to employ them.

Ever since then—and this, I think, is my only real qualification for talking to you this evening—I have been concerned with attempts to read and interpret company accounts rather than with their preparation. And it is from this angle of reading and interpretation, rather than from any technical viewpoint, that I wish to approach my task this evening.

Quite simply, what I propose to do is to describe to you the mental processes through which a financial journalist passes when a company's report and accounts are laid before him and he is required to examine and analyse them and to express an opinion on them and on the investment merits of the shares of that company.

First, I think I ought to make it plain that such a financial journalist, if he really knows his job, approaches any set of accounts with a certain degree of cynicism and suspicion. I hope this will not shock you too greatly. After all, you are the people who do, or will, certify that these accounts give a " true and fair " statement of the company's position. But frankly, quite often we just don't believe you. I am quite prepared to believe that within the terms of your definitions, you use the words " true and fair " with all sincerity. But the older a financial journalist becomes, the less does it seem to him, within the terms of *his* definitions, that many company accounts are either true or fair.

* A Lecture delivered to the Edinburgh Chartered Accountants Students' Society on February 19, 1954.

Let me give you some examples, some perfectly true examples, from real life, of what I mean. Once upon a time, there was a company which, having already passed its Ordinary dividend, was also failing to earn its Preference dividend on any realistic accounting basis. The directors knew this, and had decided privately, among themselves, that the Preference dividend would not be paid. But on the day when the normally quite formal announcement of the Preference dividend was due, it so happened that the directors were scattered far and wide. It may have been the time of the Grand National, or grouse shooting may have just started, or what have you. Whatever the reason, the secretary of the company, who was not aware of the directors' private decision taken among themselves, went ahead in the usual way and sent the announcement to the Stock Exchange that the Preference dividend would be paid. After all, why shouldn't he? It always had been paid in the past, and the whole thing to him seemed just routine.

Then, however, the directors were faced with the choice of going ahead with their original stringent plans for valuing stocks and work in progress and showing the Preference dividend unearned, or of following a more optimistic valuation and showing sufficient profits to cover the dividend. Not unnaturally, they chose the second course. In the circumstances, it is not for me to criticise them. But I mention the case to show why we financial journalists are sometimes a little cynical about company accounts.

Again, there is a famous company, whose activities are centred not a thousand miles from Edinburgh, which carries the main factory in its books at £469,002—I like the two pounds—although the chairman is on record only a year or two ago with the statement that the cost of construction was £4¼ millions, and the replacement value would be £25 millions.

You will, I think, concede that it is rather difficult, in these circumstances, to judge from that company's accounts whether earnings are adequate or not, or what the true rate of earnings on the true capital employed really is.

Quite apart from these difficulties, we realise, of course, that there are inherent limitations in any set of accounts, however truly and realistically those accounts are drawn up. A balance sheet, for example, is drawn up as at one particular day in the year. Very often, I think, the date is especially chosen, on quite legitimate grounds, to suit a company's convenience on such matters as stocktaking. However that may be, it is, I am certain, unwise to assume that because a company shows an excellent liquid position on March 31, with current assets well in excess of current liabilities, the same company will be as comfortably off on April 30. After all, it is well known that such august institutions as our big banks go in for what is known as window-dressing about the date of their accounts. No one thinks any the worse of them for so doing, but it *is* as well to appreciate the limitations imposed by these inevitable accounting traditions.

The next general point I wish to make is that in my experience a really balanced interpretation of a company's financial position cannot be made by reference to any one single set of accounts. I am not, of course, in any way belittling the value of the latest report and accounts of a company. Even to try to do so would be folly. The latest accounts are obviously the most topical and are often, although not invariably, the most important of the lot. It is in those accounts that one finds the financial outcome of the latest trading experience. It is in the latest balance sheet that one can discern, for example, whether a company will be approaching the capital market for new funds.

But to believe that you can really ascertain the development, the strength, the standing of a company, and the investment merits of its shares, from one set of accounts, even the latest, is to delude yourself. To do a thorough job, I suggest it is essential to regard the latest set of accounts as just the last of a series of perhaps ten or fifteen. And as much attention must be given to the whole series as to the latest set.

For this there are general and specific reasons. The general reasons are that a company itself is a gradually developing organism, and the manner in which it is developing, and indeed whether it is developing at all, can only be judged if, as it were, a bird's-eye view is taken of its accounts over a fairly long period. Moreover, it is of course possible that a normally very conservatively managed business may, on occasion and for perfectly valid reasons, decide to depart from its conservatism for one year. Or a business which is not conservatively managed may contrive to give a temporary appearance of conservatism which can be quite misleading.

The specific reasons are more technical. I have in mind here in particular the freedom which is given to certain of our companies, notably our shipping companies, to exempt themselves from the requirements of the general company law in the matter of full disclosure of certain aspects of their finances. I can recall cases where, with such companies, a brand new asset has been written in and written out of a balance sheet in a remarkably short space of time and afterwards no trace of the new asset, or at least no adequate trace, can be discerned in its subsequent accounts.

These, then, are some of the general considerations which will run through the mind of the analyst as he settles down with the file of a company's accounts before him. Now for the particular fashion in which he will make a detailed assessment. Does he examine first the profit and loss accounts? Or is his initial attention given to the balance sheet? I have little doubt that the general investing public concentrates most of its attention on the profit and loss account. This, it seems to them, is what really matters. How much profit has the company made? How big a dividend is it paying? Are the directors distributing approximately the same proportion of earnings in dividend? Or has there been a change in dividend policy? Do the directors seem to concern themselves unduly with their own remuneration, or with staff funds, rather than with the shareholders' pay?

These are the things on which the public concentrates, and very understandably, for they are all matters of the greatest importance. But I hope our investment analyst is more sophisticated than the general public, sufficiently sophisticated to appreciate that the profit and loss account must be read very much in conjunction with the balance sheet.

True, the profit and loss account requires its own special examination. For what a board of directors may regard as an obligatory charge against profits, the independent analyst may judge to be more suitably regarded as an optional reservation. He will be on the alert, too, for non-recurring charges and special non-recurring credits alike. He will attempt to judge, as well as an outside observer may, whether the company's taxation provision bears approximately the orthodox and expected ratio to total taxable profits, for herein he may find a very valuable clue as to the conservatism of a board of directors.

Surprisingly often we find tax provisions which seem—quite apart from such special factors as E.P.L.—to be disproportionately high, which suggests to us that the company has made charges against its profits which the tax authorities do not regard as suitable charges for tax purposes. On the other hand, we may find a tax provision which seems unduly low. A common cause of this low tax provision, of course, is past losses, and where this happens there is a big question mark over the future. What will be the position when the benefit of these past losses has been exhausted?

In fine, what the analyst is after is the closest definition he can get of the year's true profits, buttressed by whatever mental reservations he may deem to be necessary to cover what seems to be conservative provision for tax liabilities and so on. Where he has to adjust one year's official figures by reason of special credits and debits carried over from previous years, he will, with his serial picture in mind, endeavour to adjust earlier years' profits figures by carrying back and apportioning those debits and credits to the years to which they belong. This, however, is generally a very difficult process for the outside observer, although I must record the fact that when we have asked companies to apportion such figures for us over past years they have often been remarkably helpful in doing so, if indeed it is practicable for anyone to make the apportionment.

Having then obtained a series of what he regards as the truest profit figures he can obtain by means of such adjustments—if indeed they be necessary—our analyst will, of course, spend some time just studying any trends which the figures portray. He will then attempt to relate them to the assets from which they have been earned. How well he succeeds in establishing any worthwhile relationship will depend, of course, on how " historic " the balance sheet is. I can only say that quite often we find that the relating of profits to net asset values produces results of great interest and value.

I recall one case in particular. The company is well known and highly regarded. For years it had shown steady profits and been most conservative in distributing them. Indeed, over a period of six or seven years it had raised new capital and ploughed back profits into the business to the tune of no less than £2·1 million. But when we started relating the latest profits to the asset values as augmented by these issues and constant ploughings back, we found that the company was earning only 1⅜ per cent on the disclosed asset values—and certainly the figures would have been even less if we could have found the replacement values of those assets. This company, in fact, was emulating the Red Queen in ' Alice Through the Looking Glass.' It was running very fast to keep in the same place. Indeed, it was not even staying in the same place; it was slipping backwards. Its ploughings back were, in the economic sense, quite unjustified by results, and the shares, instead of the conservative blue chip they had appeared to be from a mere comparison of earnings and dividends, were now seen to be a rather indifferent holding.

I freely concede, of course, that the value of such exercises is limited by information about asset values provided in the balance sheet. But as a general proposition, this test is well worth carrying out whenever possible. And if all our companies would do what *some* of them do, and have a periodic revaluation of assets, this test would do a great deal not only to help the investment analyst but would also ensure that more of our investment was directed into the most profitable channels.

Next, I suggest the analyst casts a general eye over the balance sheet. Is the liquid position satisfactory—subject to the reservation I have already made about "one-day accounting"? How do I define "satisfactory"? I cannot—with any exactitude. It will depend on many factors. Has the company any early maturing obligations among its liabilities? Is it known to be committed to any plan for substantial expansion of fixed assets? Are commodity prices rising or falling—for this may well affect its stock requirements in the coming year? Do stocks and work in progress appear unduly high or low in relation to previous years and in relation to what is known about the trend of the company's progress? If stocks and work in progress seem high at a time when commodity prices and trade activity are falling, will not the company probably have to take losses on these items?

"Liquid assets," or "current assets" are sometimes taken to comprise three main items—stock and work in progress, marketable investments not held as trade investments, and cash. This, I suggest, is imperfect definition. At the top of the post-Korean boom, by this definition, some companies were reasonably liquid—but only because "liquid assets," or "current assets," included large investments in stock and work in progress.

In the wrong trading conditions such assets can be far from liquid or current, and I prefer to make three classifications of total assets—fixed, which include factories, plant and equipment; working, which comprise stocks and work in progress; and quick, which include realisable investments and cash. It is necessary, of course, in arriving at a net liquid asset or net quick asset position to deduct current or quick liabilities.

A word or two here about over-trading. A company may well be showing bumper profits through over-trading. This is not always easy to spot from the accounts, but if there are signs of unwieldy stocks, work in progress, debtors and creditors, combined with a deficiency of quick assets, there may be reason to suspect over-trading. This may not be disastrous but it may lead to sharp revision of dividend policy. For it is not enough to earn profits; if you'll forgive a blinding glimpse of the obvious, a company needs cash to pay dividends.

Next, perhaps I may say a little about calculating asset values per Ordinary share. I could spend a long while discussing the merits and demerits of such calculations. All I will say is that despite all the objections of the critics I have for a long time believed asset value calculations to be decidedly useful—and I would submit that recent events have justified me in that view. In making such calculations, the routine work is simple enough but I would stress that care is necessary to ascertain as closely as possible if prior charges are redeemable at a premium, or if

Preference shares have any extra participation in asset distribution above their nominal value. Checking on such facts may involve resort to a company's articles of association, which sounds a counsel of perfection, but which is something which the thorough analyst ought to do. On my experience, reference to the orthodox, public sources of reference is not enough.

I do, of course, and always have conceded that the use of the asset value calculations needs to be handled with a great deal of circumspection but I have found in the past, particularly at times of great depression or great exuberance in stock markets, that the use of asset values combined with an American technique can be highly useful in relating the story told by a set of company accounts to the price of the company's shares in the market. This American technique employs what is known as the " area of over-or-under valuation." Quite simply, what one does is to take the stock-market valuation of the business and contrast it with the net balance-sheet valuation. In times of depression in markets, one often finds that the area of under-valuation is very great. That is to say that one is paying perhaps 20s. for a share in the market when on balance-sheet values alone one is buying total net assets equivalent to 40s. a share and possibly net quick assets alone of maybe 25s. a share. On the other hand, in times of great market exuberance one may find an area of considerable over-valuation where the market price of a business is away above the balance-sheet valuation of that business. At such times one usually hears the argument that if the assets of the business were re-valued there would be no area of over-valuation. This argument has a great deal of validity but the conservative investor will prefer, in using asset values, the company where it is not necessary to call such arguments in aid.

Next perhaps I may touch upon one or two fallacies which arise in connection with the interpretation of company accounts. These fallacies, I am pleased to say, seem to me to be diminishing, but they are still a trap for some investors. Take, for example, the case of the investor who believes in a company with strong reserves. On general grounds, of course, *I* believe in a company building up strong reserves in so far as such reserves can in general only be built up by a conservative profit distribution policy. At the same time, it is always rather difficult, I think, to hold a high opinion of a company one day because it has massive reserves and the following day to think poorly of it because, by capitalising those reserves and transferring them to capital account, the company's balance sheet appears to have no reserves at all.

Similarly, there is sometimes a snag where goodwill and other intangible assets are concerned. I know investors who for years have fought shy of certain companies because their balance sheet contains substantial goodwill and other intangible items. I agree that it is preferable that such intangible assets should be written out of a balance sheet as soon as possible. At the same time, if I were in the issuing house business I could, without any difficulty at all, produce for you alternative capitalisations for the same business, one of which would show a substantial goodwill item, and the second of which would show no apparent goodwill at all. Presumably my ultra-conservative friends would say that the company in its second guise was a sound business whereas with its first capitalisation it would be regarded as a speculative and somewhat reckless undertaking.

It is also true, of course, in connection with the question of the area of over- or under-valuation to which I was referring just now, that, particularly in times of market optimism there is in fact a large element of goodwill in many of our businesses when one compares the market valuation of the business with the balance sheet valuation. I think you will find, for example, that the market valuation of Woolworths invariably, in fact whether it be in times of depression or times of exuberance, represents a very substantial item of hidden goodwill compared with the balance sheet valuation of the business. And yet I suppose during our lifetime there have been few finer investments to hold as permanent holdings than the shares of Woolworth.

In conclusion, of course, all this has to be related to the price of the share or shares of the company under examination. And it is a sobering and somewhat depressing fact that the analyst, after he has spent hours in examining and interpreting a company's accounts for a period of ten or fifteen years will find that all his conclusions are already reflected in the price of a company's shares. This is at one and the same time a salutary reminder to any analyst that many other and better brains than his have already been at work, and also a tribute to that nowadays rather unfashionable piece of machinery known as the mechanics of the marketplace. The Stock Exchange is, as you know, very widely regarded these days as nothing more than a casino or a glorified and complicated version of Littlewood's Football Pools. In fact, however, the more an analyst of company accounts persists in his work the more he is astonished at the manner in which the Stock Exchange is in reality merely a mirror reflecting the thinking of hundreds of thousands of people, who have already forestalled him. But lest you should be too depressed, I would assure you that, from my own experience, every now and again a careful analysis of company accounts on the lines which I have broadly suggested to you tonight does pay off in a big way. The market, in short, is not infallible, and patience and hard work in interpreting company accounts can be rewarded.

One final word. There is a short cut, a very short cut to the interpretation of company accounts. It is generally to be found on the first or second page of a company report and accounts and consists quite simply of the names of the directors of the business. You will not expect me to enlarge on this aspect of the matter, but I can assure you that I and, I am sure, other members of my audience tonight know very well, when we see certain names on this first or second page of a company's report, pretty well what sort of a picture the accounts will show. In fact, what I am trying to say is that, useful though analysis and interpretation of company accounts undoubtedly is, the finest way of assessing the value of a business is to know the quality—or otherwise—of its management.

For Product Safety Concerns and Information please contact our EU
representative GPSR@taylorandfrancis.com
Taylor & Francis Verlag GmbH, Kaufingerstraße 24, 80331 München, Germany

www.ingramcontent.com/pod-product-compliance
Lightning Source LLC
Chambersburg PA
CBHW052125300426
44116CB00010B/1793